THE BASICS OF THROWING

THE BASICS OF
THROWING

David Cohen

A & C Black • London
University of Pennsylvania Press • Philadelphia

First published in Great Britain in 2008
A & C Black Publishers Limited
38 Soho Square
London W1D 3HB
www.acblack.com

ISBN: 978-0-7136-8129-1

Published simultaneously in the USA by
University of Pennsylvania Press
3905 Spruce Street
Philadelphia, Pennsylvania 19104-4112
www.pennpress.org

ISBN: 978-0-8122-2041-4

Cover images (front): Various throwing images by David Cohen.
Frontispiece: Assorted images of clay and throwing by David Cohen.

Book design by Penny and Tony Mills
Cover design by James Watson

Printed and bound in China

A&C Black uses paper produced with elemental chlorine-free pulp, harvested from managed
sustainable forests.

CONTENTS

Foreword   6

Introduction   8

1   Properties of Clay and its Preparation for Use   10

2   Basic Technical Principles of the Potter's Wheel   24

3   Getting Started: Throwing Basics   28

4   Technical Vocabulary and Visual Vocabulary   48

5   The Open Form   62

6   The Discipline of Function   74

7   Rudiments of Expression   100

8   Expressive Approaches To Basic Thrown Forms   112

9   Inspiration From Source Material   128

Suppliers List   143

Index   144

FOREWORD

There are few disciplines left in the 21st century so completely devoid of technology as the experience of throwing a pot. There is something profoundly direct, immediate and totally consuming in this particular relationship between potter and clay. From the moment the clay is placed on the potter's wheel, through the controlling of motion and speed, the placing of hands, the feeling, sensing, moving, shaping, all done with total control, total concentration, there is perhaps no other material that has the ability to transform itself so immediately. By the creative use of the human hand something formless is made into a three-dimensional object of utility, even beauty.

The experience is a pure joy when all these qualities come together in an orchestrated balance of movement. It is the perfect expression of physical skill and emotional control, not unlike other disciplines such as dance, sport or music, which require a similar display to achieve performance at the highest level.

Mastering a craft requires many hours of repetitive practice and reflection, as well as knowledge, understanding and application to the task, deep desire and the will to succeed. These qualities are necessary, though they are difficult to teach, and even to truly define; they can perhaps best be summed up in the genuine enthusiasm for work. They have nothing to do with talent but contribute greatly to the ways we choose creatively to express ourselves.

There are many aspects of throwing that can't be graphically illustrated or intellectually explained. Merely reading books on the subject will leave gaps in learning, because throwing forces you into a very human place; a place of action where you become acutely aware of how challenging it is to give clay form and, perhaps most importantly, how the concept (and the reality) of time becomes central to the process of learning and achievement. Appreciating how long it will take to master even the most basic principles of throwing is perhaps the greatest challenge. To prepare physically and emotionally for the reality that progress will not be instant is important for the beginner.

There are no magical short cuts to success – special equipment, materials and tools that will make learning the basics of throwing any easier or faster. That is the difficulty but also the very thing that makes the experience so worthwhile and the eventual achievement so satisfying.

This book attempts to reflect deeply on every aspect of the throwing experience. David Cohen is a master of his craft, achieved through a work ethic that has spanned over 40 years with hardly a single day when he wasn't touching clay or thinking about it. To master clay requires this devotion. The reader can benefit from his experience by following the clear and logical analysis set out in this book, so that over time and with practice the very best foundation for success will have been laid.

Small insights related to breathing and posture are recognised and explained through a holistic perspective that realises the importance of applying the component parts incrementally to achieve the skills and understanding necessary to sustain practice.

The performance-based skill of throwing cannot be perfected in isolation from the integrity of good design. The ability to draw is never far from this outcome and should always be regarded as integral to the development of visual vocabulary. This is clearly illustrated and described throughout.

We are living in a time of immense creative diversity in art and design, where no new, recognised movement has emerged, while at the same time there is a sense of 'coming to terms with' or 'getting to know' the potential of technology. It is an interesting historical moment in art but also a confusing one. No one can say with any certainty where technology will lead or whether it will contribute anything of lasting value. Let's just say there is something reassuring in the knowledge that the craft of throwing remains true. The basics will never change; they are essential to forming a visual statement. That knowledge is great freedom.

Scott Anderson   2008

INTRODUCTION

Even after forty years' involvement with ceramics, I have never ceased to be fascinated by the craft of the potter's wheel. As a professional ceramic craftsperson and teacher within art institutions, for me analysing every aspect associated with the potter's wheel seemed an essential task. Other clay techniques – handbuilding, slipcasting, mouldmaking, press-moulding, coiling or decorating – are not comparable with working on the wheel. Through a direct relationship with the wheel itself I have been able to investigate the movement, spontaneity and agility associated with throwing.

Trial and error can be an extremely frustrating experience for the beginner. It is essential that certain principles of mechanics associated with the potter's wheel are understood before any attempt to create a form is undertaken. With an understanding of these mechanical principles the novice will be able to relate the process of throwing a form to the physical position of the body and hands when doing so. The introduction to throwing must be consistent with this process and directly affiliated with the physical position, mental attitude and rhythm. It would be a great injustice to the teaching of throwing if the entire process was focused only on what the hands were doing in creating a form.

The physical relationship of the body to the wheel is of paramount importance. If tension and stress factors when seated at the wheel have not been identified, ailments such as back pains and neck problems can result. Within the following chapters tensions and stress points will be clarified to help prevent long-term physical damage.

In many parts of the world potters spend long periods each day doing repetitive throwing as part of their daily routine. When I established my pottery studio in 1964, I threw, on average, 200 mugs a day entirely on a kick wheel. It was essential that an attitude of mental and physical endurance was developed. In particular, I recognised the need for a feeling of rhythm in order to maintain production output. The physical work on the wheel for long periods of time, along with the mental attitude associated with the critical assessment of each piece thrown, were governed by the rhythm applied to the task in hand. The application of critical thought and emotional and physical response is fundamental to the ultimate success and enjoyment of creating ceramics on the potter's wheel.

Physical involvement, mental attitude and a sense of rhythm need to be defined in relation to the mechanical instrument (the potter's wheel) rotating a piece of clay at variable speeds. Physically, the problem of centring the clay will be analysed and understood through rotation and the mechanics associated with the principles of centrifugal force. The importance of posture in alleviating possible injury is an extremely important issue. If injury does occur it will have a detrimental effect not only on the body but also on the mental focus applied to assessment. This book, with the help of photographs, will address this in detail so that ultimately physical involvement and mental attitude are conceived as a single unit. Only when the physical, critical and emotional concepts are experienced, and then become part of the subconscious, can the fundamentals of design be applied. The technical basics of throwing and the principles of design should not be considered as being separate; they are an integrated unit.

There is no magical way of speeding up a process that is essentially a combination of many individual movements that ultimately, with practice and dedication, are to be experienced as one. I cannot overemphasise that, in the beginning, learning the rudiments of the potter's wheel will be very slow and to a degree tedious. I have seen beginners' wheel work that was no more than a hole made in the middle of a piece of clay, accepted as finished and ready to be fired. I sincerely hope the reader of this book will take the instruction seriously and devote time and energy to a craft that is entirely unique and a pure joy to experience.

David Cohen   2008
www.pitclaygallery.co.uk
www.davidcohenceramicartist.co.uk

1

PROPERTIES OF CLAY AND ITS PREPARATION FOR USE

Clay from the earth, plus water, air and fire are the essential elements associated with the creation and permanence of ceramics. Each one of these elements is dependent on the others in the making and finishing process. Clay needs water for workability, air for drying, and fire for permanency. But beyond this apparently simple explanation a great deal of investigation is needed to appreciate how and why these elements interact with each other, giving a variety to the finished product. With the addition of water alone, clay is capable of being formed by hand without the aid of tools. It is essentially formless yet used to create countless forms. It is also reusable time and time again if not fired. I cannot think of another material which is as flexible, as easily found, and as able to be reconstituted so simply. For all of these reasons, for me, clay is magic.

Origin of clay

The clay we use today originally began as granite and feldspathic rock; through weathering and decomposition over millions of years we have a workable material. There are two geological classifications of clay – primary and secondary. The most important primary clay is kaolin (china clay). This is found where it was initially formed. China clay is without impurities and is used to give whiteness and strength in high-fired clay bodies including porcelain. China clay has a relatively large particle size and is therefore less plastic. Bentonite, which is classified as the next most important primary clay, has a smaller particle size and can be added to a clay body to increase its plasticity. Secondary clays, which can also be called sedimentary clays, were removed from their position of origin by water and ice. Through the action of movement, abrasion, frost and weathering, the particle sizes of the secondary clays are smaller and therefore more plastic. This movement also allowed impurities to be introduced into these clays, affecting their colour both before and after firing. The most common impurity is iron oxide, which can give a distinctive range of browns to reds through the firing process.

The most useful book I have found in dealing with characteristics of ceramics is *The Potter's Dictionary of Materials and Techniques* by Frank and Janet Hamer (second edition), published by A&C Black. The description of materials and techniques is extremely comprehensive and very easy to follow for the beginner and beyond.

Beginning the investigation process

Figs 1 & 1A: 25 cm (10 in) below the topsoil is a layer of secondary clay. This clay differs from the topsoil in being denser and without the abundance of decomposed organic material. The clay will probably feel damp, being beneath the porous topsoil that allows the rainwater to reach the layer of clay.

A basic starting point is to learn to recognise clay wherever it may appear. This may be in your own garden below the topsoil, along river banks, in ploughed fields or exposed cliff faces, or in excavations of building sites and new roads.

There are basically three ways of acquiring clay: finding your own clay source and refining it yourself; mixing your own clay recipe from commercially refined dry materials; or purchasing already wet, packed clay which is ready to use.

Fig 2: These bags contain clay which has been commercially refined. All foreign matter, such as stones, sand, and organic materials, has been removed. A clay recipe can be mixed to suit the requirements of the user.

Fig 2A: This machine is an ex-bakery dough mixer. It is ideal for mixing the clay simply by adding 30% water, making it suitable for throwing on the potter's wheel or for other forms of ceramic fabrication.

Fig 3 & 3A: This picture shows a commercial way of processing clay. All the foreign materials, such as stones, sand and organic materials, are extracted by mixing the clay with a large quantity of water and then pumping it through fine-mesh screens into a filter press (blue arrow), where the surplus water is pressed out of the clay into square sheets (yellow arrow).

The clay is then put through a de-airing pug ready to be used (red arrow) for ceramic production or placed in plastic bags (see **Fig 3A**) and sold to individuals, institutions or factories.

Fig 4, 5 & 6: This is secondary clay dug from the garden. As noted in the caption to image **1A** there was a certain amount of moisture in the clay. Simply by taking a handful and squeezing, it held together, an indication that there may be enough clay particles to pursue the following procedure of refinement.

Fig 7: A large amount of water is combined with the sample from the garden and left for an hour or so. This enables the clay particles to become completely saturated. If the clay sample is completely dry, less soaking time is necessary, 10–15 minutes. When clay is in a dry state, it is very easy for the water to break, or slake, the clay down quickly. What remains are the non-absorbent materials like stones and sand.

Fig 8: A vigorous stir of all the materials is necessary before trying to sieve the sample batch. All the material is quite heavy, and probably 40 to 60% is sand and stone. These need to be eliminated for the making process, especially for throwing on the potter's wheel.

Fig 9: A 30-mesh sieve (30 being the number of holes per linear inch) is a good starting point. This will take most of the large non-clay materials out of the sample batch.

Fig 10: The debris found in the first sieving is discarded. Even though the process of refining a sample of found clay is laborious and time-consuming, it helps to appreciate the effort involved in all clay refining, whether self-made or commercially refined.

Fig 11: Pour the sieved material back into a bucket for another sieving through a finer-meshed screen.

Fig 12: The next size should be a 60-mesh screen to eliminate most of the coarse sand. Then a 120-mesh screen is used to extract the finest of non-plastic materials.

Fig 13: The remaining material after sieving through the 120-mesh sieve is all workable clay. For the clay particles to have gone through the sieving process, a considerable amount of water will have had to be used. It is advisable to leave the bucket to rest overnight. The next day, a layer of clean water will appear. Decant as much of the water as possible without losing the clay.

Fig 14: A dry plaster slab is prepared for drying the sieved clay (see pp.18–19); a clay wall is constructed around the perimeter of the plaster slab. Make sure it is pressed firmly to the plaster to prevent the liquid clay from leaking out.

Fig 15: With the clay particles being completely saturated with water the clay will remain in suspension for a long time. Once the sieved clay is poured onto the dry plaster slab the water will be absorbed very quickly.

Fig 16: Because the clay has been spread evenly over the plaster slab, it will not take long before the excess water disappears from the surface. At this point the retaining wall can be removed.

Fig 17: The clay will be easily lifted from the surface of the plaster if it is not too soft.

Fig 18: If the clay is still too soft for throwing, roll it together and flatten it again on the plaster slab. Periodically turn the clay over until the desired hardness is achieved.

Fig 19: Take a small piece of the clay and roll it out.

Fig 20: Wrapping the clay around your finger will indicate its plasticity. Make sure the clay is relatively soft. Stiff clay has a tendency to crack even though it may be quite plastic.

Fig 21: The refined clay can now be tested on the potter's wheel.
Fig 22: This clay is the same as in illustration 21. A rolling pin and two sticks of the same thickness are used to roll out a strip of clay.

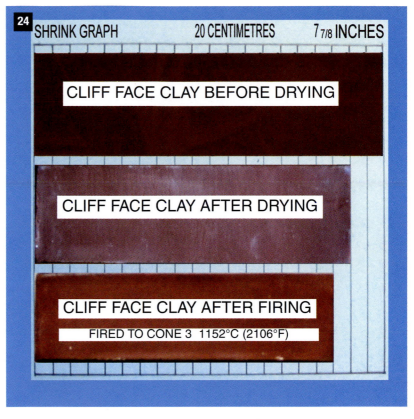

Fig 23: The final test deals with porosity. This determines if the clay is still capable of absorbing water after firing. The clay sample is weighed when it is removed from the kiln. It is then put into a bowl of water for 24 hours and weighed again. This will determine if the clay has absorbed any water. The firing temperature and the porosity are related to each other. With this sample, the clay weighed the same after a 24-hour soaking as it did when removed from the kiln. The clay can now be classified as being completely vitreous, or incapable of absorbing water.

Fig 24: The clay strip is laid on a grid divided into 20 cm (7⅞ in). Note the shrinkage not only in length but also in width. The bottom strip has been fired to 1152°C (2106°F). The colour change between each of the three stages is also very distinctive.

This concludes the basic testing procedure for self-found clay.

The process of finding and refining clay can be very rewarding. On the other hand, energy may be better applied to practising the craft of the potter's wheel than to the effort of processing found clay, which in any case would be needed in considerable quantity. Ready-made clay from a commercial clay producer is the most sensible way of beginning an involvement with ceramics.

Plaster slab-making and clay-wedging for the potter's wheel

In institutions, industry and well-equipped ceramic studios there will be machinery such as pug mills, filter presses and mixing apparatus to reconstitute scrap clay. As stated earlier, I cannot think of another material that can be used over and over again without losing its original identity.

No matter how big or small production may be, the plaster slab is an invaluable asset. The following illustrations show how to make a plaster slab.

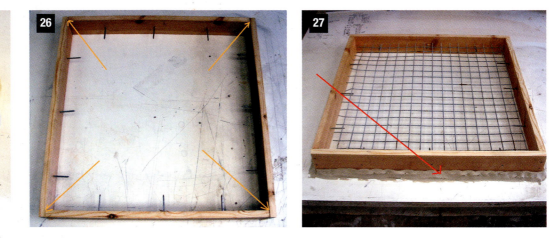

Fig 25: A good casting surface should be non-porous (e.g. plastic-coated board). A light coating of washing-up liquid over the casting area is needed to stop the slab from sticking to the surface when it is finally removed.

Fig 26: A wooden frame 46 cm (18 in) square by 6 cm (2½ in) deep is a reasonable size; 1.5 cm (⅝ in) is sufficient thickness for the wood. The corners of the frame are nailed or screwed together (orange arrows). Nails are driven through the frame to prevent the plaster slipping out of it. The wooden frame also protects the edges of the plaster from chipping.

Fig 27: A piece of wire mesh is desirable to help prevent cracking of the slab. Plaster does not have a great deal of structural strength. A clay seal around all four sides is essential to prevent the plaster running out of the wooden frame (red arrow).

Fig 28: Measure the amount of water in relation to the area to be covered. The first pour will fill the wooden frame half full. Nine pints of water (6 litres) is the approximate quantity of water needed.

Fig 29: Fine casting plaster is used because it sets fairly fast. Potters' plaster, sold for mould-making, is also suitable. Pottery supply companies furnish these products (use a 25 kg / 56 lb bag). If all the plaster is not used once the bag is open, make sure the remaining plaster is put into a plastic bag, sealed tight and stored in a dry place. Plaster does not have a long shelf life. Even though it is sealed tight, and in a dry place, six months is about its limit. After that it will start to develop small lumps and when mixed with water will set extremely fast.

Fig 30: The dry plaster is *always* added to the water, not the other way around. Put the water into a clean bucket and add the plaster very slowly. This is to let the plaster particles be saturated with water more quickly. Keep pouring plaster into the water until you see little islands appear on the surface.

Fig 31: After letting the plaster absorb water for a few minutes, stir vigorously from the bottom of the bucket. Stirring by hand is essential to determining when the plaster has properly thickened; it should be the consistency of double cream. This process takes a bit of time, so do not be impatient. Remember to keep stirring from the bottom of the bucket.

Fig 32: At this point pour the plaster into the wooden frame from one point and let the plaster flow across the bottom. Remember that 9 pints of water were adjudged to fill only half of the slab up to the wire mesh. The reason for doing only half the slab is so as to be more able to calculate how much plaster to mix for the top pour.

Fig 33: The first pour of plaster is left to harden, and any plaster over the mesh should be roughened up, enabling the second pour to adhere to the first pour.

Fig 34: The second pour is filled to the top of the wooden frame and slightly above. It is important to let the plaster set to cream-cheese hardness, though not beyond at this stage.

Fig 35: At this point a straight edge is pulled along the wooden frame and the surplus plaster is removed. In the setting process, the plaster swells up, and it may be necessary to pull the straight edge more than once.

Fig 36: For the next 20 minutes the plaster will become very warm to the touch. Once the plaster and water are mixed together, a chemical reaction occurs as the plaster hardens. When the plaster is very hard to the touch, a metal rib can be used to smooth the surface if desired, but this is not altogether necessary. The other side of the slab should be very smooth – ideal for absorbing water from the clay. The slab contains 17 pints of water, 9 from the first pour and 8 from the second. All this water will have to evaporate before the slab is usable. Any warm environment where it can be left for a period of time will do.

With the assistance of the plaster slab, the procedure of wedging and preparing clay for the potter's wheel can be demonstrated. Even though access to a pug mill may be available, the extraction of water from slop clay is still necessary.

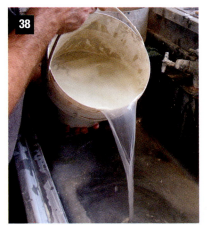

Fig 37: All unfired dry clay and slop can be put into a bucket. Submerse everything in water and let it stand overnight.

Fig 38: Decant as much of the clear water as possible.

Fig 39: The slop clay is then put onto the plaster slab to extract the excess water.

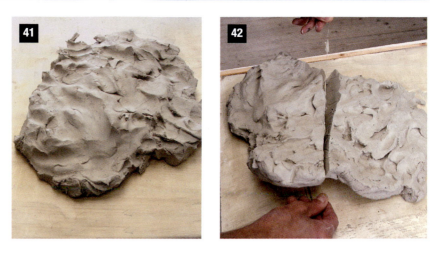

Fig 40: Spread out the clay and leave until the underside is firm enough that the clay can be turned over.

Fig 41: The clay should remain quite soft, ready to be put through a pug mill or wedged by hand (see Fig 53–7). There are two types of pug mills, de-airing and non de-airing.

Fig 42: Begin by cutting the clay in half.

Fig 43: One half is placed on top of the other.

Fig 44: Both pieces are picked up together.

Fig 45: These pieces are turned one quarter.

Fig 46: The clay is put down on the slab with the front portion up (red arrow).

Fig 48: Illustration 40 shows lumps of clay and slop clay mixed together. In order for this clay to be reused on the potter's wheel, the mass must be completely homogeneous. To illustrate this very important point, the white clay and the brown clay will be wedged together.

Fig 47: This allows the cutting wire to be placed underneath the clay with ease (blue arrow). This process of cutting and turning is continued until the softer and harder clays are integrated.

Fig 49: This is after two cuts with a quarter turn each time.

Fig 50: The brown clay and the white clay are starting to become integrated through continuous cutting and turning.

Fig 51: This illustration demonstrates they are now one colour and of the same hardness throughout, i.e. suitable for throwing.

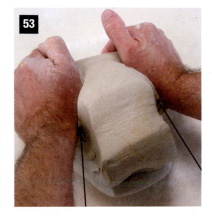

Fig 52: A good-quality board 1.5 cm (⅝ in) thick, covered with a heavy-weight canvas, is ideal for wedging and other applications. Clay which is ready for throwing or handbuilding does not stick to this surface and will not stiffen the clay as readily as would the plaster slab.

Fig 53: This method of wedging is known as the 'ram's head'. The clay is pushed forward and inwards on the first movement (black arrows).

Fig 54: The next movement is pulling the clay upwards and repeating the movement downwards and inwards as in illustration 53.

Fig 55: The other method of wedging is a rolling motion caused by lifting the clay up and pushing it down.

Fig 56: The trick is to keep the clay on the same spot as you roll and push.

Fig 57: No matter what the method is, rolling or the ram's head, they both take practice until they become second nature.

The introduction to clay and its preparation has had a single purpose – to introduce clay to the maker in a basic and understandable way. It is important for the maker to associate clay with the elements of water, air and fire. Once extracted from the earth these three elements have a profound effect on the clay's physical condition, which is directly associated with its workability. The nature of these elements can vary the feel of the clay in subtle ways. Anyone using clay will gain a respect for the material as they become more sensitive to how it reacts when used to create a form, whether on the potter's wheel or via other methods.

2 BASIC TECHNICAL PRINCIPLES OF THE POTTER'S WHEEL

Before attempting to place a piece of clay on the potter's wheel for the first time, it is important to understand some basic mechanical principles of the wheel that will contribute to your success when you begin to throw. To understand the mechanics of the potter's wheel is to understand the principles related to the wheel's movement and the movement of clay on the wheel. There are two principal types of wheel design both (kick wheel and electric wheel) serving similar purposes related to preference, comfort and speed control.

Fig 58: A shaft (green arrow), wheel head (red arrow) and flywheel (blue arrow) held rigid by a frame is an extremely basic concept. The Egyptians were the first to be credited with its use as early as 3000BC. Their wheel would have used the same basic components, though made of wood. (Designed by Paul Soldner.)

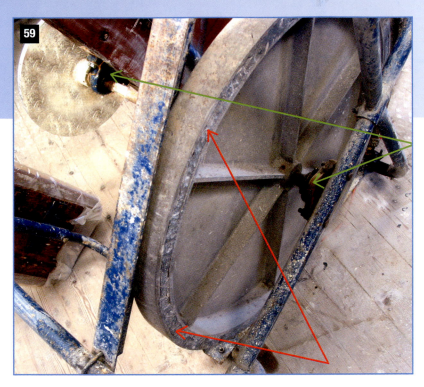

Fig 59: The modern potter's wheel has precision ball bearings for smoothness (green arrows) and cast aluminium components (flywheel and wheel head). The outer edge of the flywheel is filled with lead to give extra weight, creating maximum efficiency through centrifugal force (red arrows).

Fig 60: The body is seated in a comfortable position, leaving the legs free to kick on the flywheel as illustrated in pictures 60 & 61. From the seated position the wheel head is about level with the transitional point where the legs meet the torso, which is also shown in illustration 65.

Fig 61: The body should be relaxed and the kicking motion on the flywheel should be effortless (more like a running motion). Sitting in a comfortable and free position is essential when long periods of throwing are necessary.

Fig 62: The flywheel's weight maintains enough momentum for the form to be developed without having to kick the flywheel in the middle of a lift. To stop the wheel for any reason, pressure on the heel of the right foot will be a sufficient brake (red arrow).

Fig 63: The entire structure of this kick wheel is made of wood, including the flywheel. The potter sits in a saddle position (red arrow).

The chain has two functions. It is attached to a horizontal piece of wood, which acts as a pedal to push the flywheel around, and secondly, the chain can be adjusted to raise or lower the pedal according to the potter's size and comfort (blue arrow).

Fig 64: The lower part of the shaft is offset, and attached directly to the flywheel without a bearing (red arrow). The upper part of the shaft remains in line to revolve the wheel head (green arrow). This system requires the wooden horizontal pedal to be pushed continuously back and forth; the faster the pedal is pushed back and forth, the faster the wheel head will revolve (blue arrow).

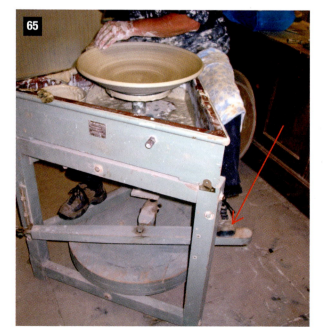

Fig 65: This potter, Brian Shand, works on a Leach-style wheel, and here concentrates on making the bowl form while his left foot (red arrow) is constantly pushing back and forth.

Both kick wheels serve the same purpose, though via a different driving action. One is not better than the other; they simply have a different mechanical solution to make the wheel head rotate. In both cases the wheel heads are held firmly in place by a smooth-running bearing. Thus the same basic principles govern both types of potter's wheels.

Fig 66: This is a modern motor-driven potter's wheel. The basic principle of the drive mechanism is the same as for the kick wheels; for smooth running the wheel head is held firmly in place by a bearing housing.

The shaft has a belt-driven wheel connected to it (blue arrow). This wheel in turn is connected by the belt (green arrows) to the motor (red arrow). At the motor end the belt feeds around a small wheel measuring 2.5 cm (1 in). At the shaft end, the belt-driven wheel is 25.5 cm (10 in). The larger wheel attached to the wheel head rotates once, while the small wheel on the motor performs ten revolutions in the same time. The foot pedal (yellow arrow) controls the speed of the wheel head from 0 to 250 revolutions per minute, giving the potter complete control when throwing. This type of wheel will be used in the chapter on throwing large forms.

The descriptions in the above illustrations explain the differences in the mechanical design of each wheel, and yet they all have a common mechanical principle. The wheel head and the driving mechanism (flywheel, pedal or motor) are held firmly on a rigid frame and connected together by a shaft or belt.

chapter 3

GETTING STARTED: THROWING BASICS

The following describes an introduction to the throwing process, essentially, how successfully to throw a cylinder form on the wheel. This process is always related to the mechanical principles of the wheel in rotation. It must be emphasised that, for the beginner, successfully mastering the cylinder is the cornerstone for successfully being able to throw all forms and thus being able to communicate your intentions when throwing.

After reading this chapter you will understand intellectually how to throw a cylinder, but please appreciate that it will take many hours of repetitive practice on the wheel to master it physically. 'Practice makes perfect', goes the saying, and that is true in this case. You will need determination, perseverance and enthusiasm for the task, qualities that cannot be taught.

After hours of repetitive practice, carefully putting into action the following principles, you will be able to:

■ Prepare a piece of clay for throwing   29

■ Maintain correct physical posture when throwing   29

■ Understand wheel mechanics and centring principles   31

■ Centre a piece of clay   32

■ Open the form   35

■ Create the base   36

■ Complete first lift   37

■ Understand the mechanics of lifting   39

■ Apply second lift: correct finger position   41

■ Apply third (final) lift (and avoid common mistakes)   42

■ Remove the finished work from the wheel   45

■ Work in series: feel rhythm and assess work   47

Prepare a piece of clay for throwing

Fig 67: For the beginner to place an irregular piece of clay (as shown above) on the wheel in readiness to throw a pot would make centring the clay very difficult.

1.1 kg (2½ lb) is a reasonable amount of clay to begin with.

Fig 68: Holding a piece of clay in one hand and patting it with the other hand until it is a conical shape is easy to do.

Fig 69: This cone form is ideal for placing on the wheel head. It is almost symmetrical and will make the centring process much easier. At the beginning the centring process will take concentration and perseverance.

Correct physical posture

Fig 70: The cone-shaped clay is placed as close to the centre of the wheel as possible, minimising the effort needed to centre the clay.

Tools List (see also p.44)

- Cutting wire
- Sponge
- Shaping rib
- Base trimmer
- Trimming needle
- Stick sponge

Fig 71: There are two major problems that beginners encounter. The first is using clay which is too stiff. The second is having the arms pressed tightly to the sides of the torso: this gives a false sense of security and will lead to many problems when lifting the clay to form a cylinder.

The right arm rests gently on the right thigh (red arrow). (If you are left-handed, as above, the main force will be from the left, and the right hand will guide.) The left arm (blue arrow) is held *away* from the torso. The hands will be withdrawn from the clay whenever the feet push the flywheel around (see illustrations 60 & 61).

Fig 72: The exact opposite is illustrated here. This potter is right-handed and the main force is on that side (blue arrow). With this type of wheel, the left arm is lightly resting on the edge of the splash pan (red arrow). Looking at this illustration, the potter looks quite relaxed.

At first the centring process will feel very awkward. Avoid sitting at the wheel for long periods of time; half-hour intervals will be sufficient at the beginning. Relax and reflect on your progress, then try again.

The following discussion takes the beginner through the centring procedure step by step.

Wheel mechanics and centring principles

The description in chapter 2 of the potter's wheels and their mechanical similarities should not be ignored: the mechanics of the wheel and the throwing procedure, from centring to the construction of a well-made cylinder, must be thought of as being inseparable from each other. The following illustrations will, time and time again, refer to the mechanics of the wheel in relation to movements of the hands as well as positions of the body.

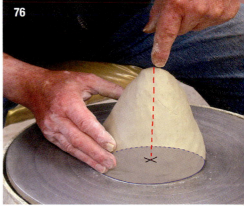

Fig 73: If there is any suspicion that the wheel is not standing level, put a builder's level on the wheel head in both directions as shown. If it is not level, the form will not stand straight when it is cut from the wheel head.

Fig 74: As already mentioned, when rotating, the wheel head and the flywheel are held firmly in position by a rigid frame. This has been mentioned before. The following illustrations and descriptions will identify why this is so important.

Fig 75: There is no way of understanding how a piece of clay is centred without first understanding one of the fundamental principles of mechanics related to rotation, namely, *during rotation, what happens on one side automatically happens on the other side*. If a black marker is placed on one point of a rotating wheel head, in order to draw a complete circle the marker should not move. This principle of the drawn circle is applied to the task of centring a piece of clay.

Fig 76: The imaginary centre running through the clay cone down to the wheel head is also very important. This imaginary centre will eventually be sensed instinctively as throwing skills are developed.

Centring

Centring clay on the potter's wheel is about feel, sensitivity and movement. Feeling, sensitivity and movement are the core elements of throwing. When applied expertly these make involvement with the potter's wheel a joyful experience. The following illustrations will take the beginner through a step-by-step procedure, demonstrating the relevance of feeling, sensitivity and movement in producing a well-constructed cylinder.

Fig 77: The cone-shaped clay is carefully placed on the centre of the wheel head. The right hand is placed in a position which allows the pressure to be applied in one direction, towards the imaginary centre, keeping in mind at all times the mantra, *'During rotation, what happens on one side automatically happens on the other side'*. Using ***very soft clay*** the beginner can also try putting pressure on the clay, as shown above, without using the other hand (left-handed beginners do the same from the opposite side). In most countries the potter's wheel revolves in an anticlockwise direction; in Japan the wheel turns clockwise. But, no matter what the direction is, the principles of mechanics in relation to rotation are the same.

Fig 78: Try to avoid letting the hand slip around in either direction (black arrows). All centring depends upon the pressure being constant, parallel, and from one direction towards the imaginary centre.

Fig 79: It is now evident that the clay is centred. The exercise of gently pushing very soft clay with one hand towards the imaginary centre demonstrates that one hand is always dominant in the centring process. Notice the bottom of the clay also looks centred.

Fig 80: Approximately 1 kg (2¼ to 2½ lb) of clay is sufficient to practise centring. Both hands are on the clay in what is the normal position. The right hand is pushing towards the imaginary centre (blue line) at a 45-degree angle, while the left hand is only a guide. The left hand does not compete with the right hand. It does not push the clay in any direction, but merely steadies it (green arrow). It is very important the thumb and the fifth finger are in the positions illustrated. These two fingers help prevent the clay from drifting off centre at the points of the red arrows.

Fig 81: Instead of the clay being directed towards the imaginary centre with a downward movement from one side (as in illustration 80), the clay is now lifted with both hands. The pressure is equal from both sides upwards (red arrows). This consolidates and centralizes, but it is too tall and narrow to be easily opened to make a hollow form.

Fig 82: The pressure is repeated downwards with the right hand, as described in illustration 80 (red arrows). The left hand, which steadies the clay, also prevents the clay at the bottom from drifting outwards beyond what is intended (blue arrow).

Fig 83: If the clay is not quite centred and the dominant hand (either right or left) applies pressure directly from the top (red arrow), the bottom of the clay will remain uncentred (yellow marks). The direction of pressure is always at a 45-degree angle towards the imaginary centre (see illustration 80). (This statement has been repeated over and over because of its fundamental importance.)

Fig 84: Even though precaution has been taken to exert pressure at the right angle, the bottom of the clay may still be slightly off centre. By pulling gently with both hands from the rear (red arrows) and then holding steady, the clay should have a more centred feel. The principle that what happens on one side during rotation will automatically happen on the other is again relevant in this case. The thumbs control the top of the form in preparation for the opening procedure (blue arrows).

Illustrations 75 to 84 deal with the centring procedure and should be considered as a checklist in the learning process. A lot of practice is needed to acquire the feeling, sensitivity and movement needed to be able to properly centre the clay every time. If the clay is not truly centred, all the movements of opening and lifting will be adversely affected. At first, things will inevitably go wrong, which is why the checklist is so important. For the beginner, the clay must be very soft in order not to impose an unnecessary amount of resistance, as stiff clay would do. *As a beginner, do not use clay with grog, sand or molochite under 120-mesh size*. The parts of the hands riding on the wheel head in the initial centring will suffer from abrasion, which can become very painful. These materials are as hard as the wheel head itself and can only be pressed into the flesh as the wheel head rotates. It is not felt in the clay to the same degree because the hard material is in the soft clay. As you develop a centring technique so your sensitivity of feel will prevent abrasion from occurring, and you can begin to use coarser materials if desired.

Opening the form

Fig 85: Up to this point, all instruction has been based on using a solid piece of clay. But the centring was only a first step towards the ultimate goal of making a well-formed cylinder. In order to accomplish that goal, the solid mass of clay must be opened from the middle outwards. 'What happens on one side during rotation automatically happens on the other side' applies as equally to the opening as it does to centring. The principle is exactly the same, only in reverse. The thumb (red arrow) works from the centre outwards in one direction while the clay is restrained from drifting off centre by the left hand (blue arrows).

Fig 86: Using the indentation the thumb has made (illustration 85) the right hand is shifted so that the fingers replace the position of the thumb. The left hand is placed on top of the right hand (blue arrow) to steady it as the fingers press downwards and across the base (red arrows).

Creating the base

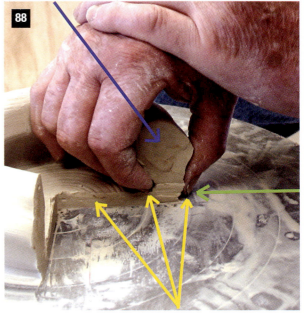

Fig 87: The right-hand fingers are drawn across the clay, opening the form and then curling underneath to create a doughnut shape (yellow arrows).

Fig 88: The thumb (green arrow) of the right hand serves two purposes. Firstly, as the inner fingers create the undercut, the thumb is held firm, not allowing the form to be dragged out further than intended. Secondly, the thumb rides on the wheel head and helps judge the thickness between the inside level and the wheel head (yellow arrows).* The bulk of the clay (blue arrow) is above the base of the form due to the undercut created by the inner fingers and the thumb.

* (Another way of assessing the thickness of the base will be illustrated in the chapter on the open form, see p.68.)

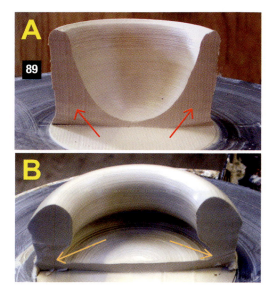

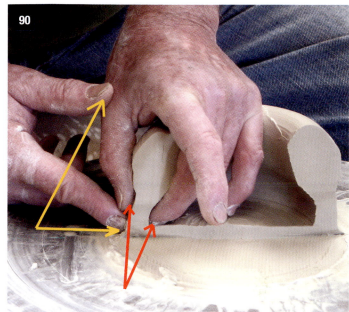

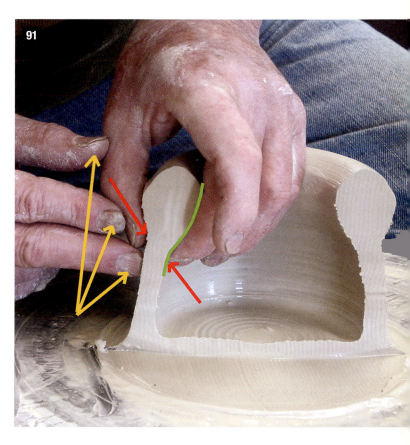

Fig 89: The top illustration (A) is typical of the inside of a beginner's form. Most of the clay remains at the bottom when the clay is opened (red arrows).

In illustration B the majority of the clay is above the bottom (yellow arrows), giving the hand a firm grip of the clay to be raised.

Fig 90: The wheel is rotating anticlockwise, so the left hand works from the inside of the form. The fingers of the left hand grip the clay at the bottom (red arrows), ready to lift it. The fingers of the right hand work together, with the left hand merely acting as a guide, contributing very little to the lifting process (yellow arrows).

Fig 91: On the first lift, the thumb and the third finger of the left hand are doing all the work, lifting and extending the cylinder with an even wall from the base (red arrows). The right hand is free to change positions if necessary, as the left hand lifts the clay (yellow arrows). Notice the position of the third finger of the left hand. It lies alongside the inner wall. This position is very important for allowing the clay to slip through the hand without ripping off the top of the form (green line).

Fig 92: Illustrations 87–91 have focused on the position of the hands in relation to what happens on the inside and outside of the form.

The above illustrates a problem that contributes to the top of the form being ripped off from the base when the third and fourth fingers of the left hand are curled under the lift (yellow line). The relationship of these fingers to the clay is very important, as shown in illustration 91 (green line).

Fig 93: The fingers inside and outside the form have now been demonstrated in relation to the first lift.

From this point onwards the body position is just as important as the position of the hands.

Fig 94: The two hands work together, with equal pressure from both sides forming a conical shape. As pressure is exerted, the hands also move upwards.

Fig 95: Illustration 90 shows the position of the left hand, both inside and out. The thumb on the outside and the other three fingers on the inside will easily reach the bottom of the form.

Fig 96: The speed of the wheel is related to the speed of the lift. As a beginner it is better to have the wheel revolve slowly in order to keep maximum control over the lifting process.

Fig 97: The free movement of the arms is the most important element in experiencing lift. The arms at this stage may be resting on the thighs, though not locked against them. It is essential to build up a vocabulary of touch that you can rely on whenever the centring, opening, lifting and forming process goes wrong. Besides the assessment of touch related to the lifting, you will also need to evaluate tension throughout the body. Holding your breath is a common reaction for the novice, but this also contributes to tension.

The mechanics of lifting

Fig 98: Throwing is not altogether a matter of speed; at the beginning it is a matter of control. Control and the sensation of lift are the two basic elements that the beginner should strive to relate to the feelings of touch and movement. Because of movement (the rotation of the clay), the sensitivity of feeling is crucial. A moderate speed of lift will be easier to control than a fast one. Another mechanical principle is centrifugal force related to speed. This means the faster the speed of the wheel, the more the clay will have a tendency to be thrown outwards, which can have an adverse effect on the making of the cylinder. The picture shows the form being conical. Because this is the first lift, it is important not to allow the form to be wider at the top than it is at the base. Experienced throwers use centrifugal force as an advantage in throwing large round forms. (This is illustrated in the chapter on large throwing.)

Fig 99: The first lift of the cylinder is cut in half from the base to the top with a wire. This will give an indication of the evenness of the cylinder walls (yellow arrows). Until the walls of the first lift can be made evenly with some consistency, there is no point in proceeding to the second and third lifts.

Fig 100: The position of the left arm in relation to the lifting procedure is extremely important. The following simple exercise will demonstrate why this is so relevant. Fill a sizeable container with water. Place the hand underneath and try raising it upwards. You will find it will wobble and feel very insecure when you push the container up from the bottom.

Figs 101 & 102: Take the same container and put it on the wheel head. Lift it by the handle upwards. Even though it is heavy, it will not wobble or feel insecure. To lift the container as described above is to introduce a feeling of lift instead of it being pushed from the bottom upwards (see illustration 100).

Fig: 103 The left arm will take the above position in order to assist the lifting of the clay. It is completely free from any support. The left arm will remain in this position throughout the second and third lifts.

Fig 104: Another reason for the left arm being in a raised position is that the left-hand fingers can no longer work from inside and outside the cylinder at the same time as they did in the first lift (see illustration 91).

Fig 105: The right-hand index finger is positioned on the outside wall of the cylinder (red arrow). The third and fourth fingers of the left hand push outwards over the index finger of the right hand to secure a grip on the clay (blue arrow).

Fig 106: The two hands work in conjunction with each other. The left arm is elevated. The wheel should revolve slowly so that you can feel the lifting process.

Third (final) lift (same as second lift)

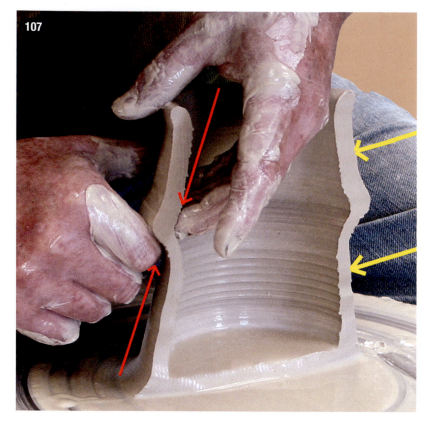

Fig 109: This is the beginning of the third lift. The left arm is held in a vertical position (see illustration 103) and the right hand moves freely upwards to form a slightly conical cylinder.

Figs 110, 111 & 112: These four illustrations (including 109) show the third lift of a conical cylinder. The speed of the wheel is relatively slow, to prevent centrifugal force throwing the clay outwards. The cylinder has a strong visual look of being stretched upwards, which relates directly to the container being lifted by the handle rather then being pushed up from the bottom (illustrations 101, 102 & 103).

Fig 107: The cylinder from the previous illustration has been cut in half, showing the relationship of both hands to each other (red arrows). The right hand lifts in conjunction with the left hand without the right hand pushing inwards or the left pushing outwards. The two hands work together with a feeling of lifting rather than pushing from the bottom upwards. The yellow arrows show the difference in wall thickness. As the hands lift the clay vertically, the bottom half of the cylinder is thinner than the top.

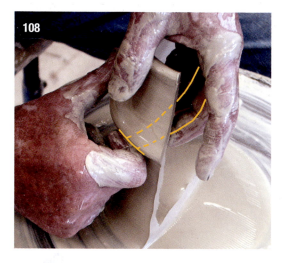

Fig 108: The index finger of the right hand is held in this position to give a broad area of contact with the clay in relation to the third and fourth fingers of the left hand on the inside of the cylinder. However, unlike the same technique in first lift pictured in illustration 92, this time *do not* curl the inside fingers.

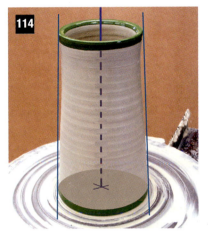

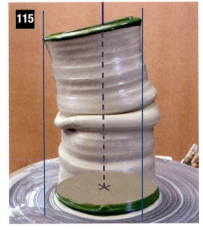

Fig 113: The wall thickness of the cylinder after the third lift is even from bottom to top. The amount of clay used in the demonstration of the conical cylinder was 1 kg (2¼ lb). This amount of clay is ideal for practising the basics of throwing. It also gives a guideline to height and width to be practised. In this case, the finished height is 21 cm (8¼ in). The height is related to the diameter of the base (12.5 cm/5 in). If the base was wider the height would be shorter. Remember, *the clay should be on the soft side in the early stages of practice*. In order to assess the consistency of height and width, the clay pieces should all be of the same weight.

Fig 114: For a beginner, it will be difficult to bring hands, arms, body and mind together with controlled movements in order to construct a well-made cylinder. Because the bottom of the cylinder is attached to the wheel head, and the top is free to move in any direction, it is very important that the imaginary centre line is consciously being considered as the clay is being lifted. *The top orbit should always be in the same parallel orbit as the bottom.*

Fig 115: This can happen when the top orbit is revolving in a different orbit from the bottom. This problem usually occurs in the final stages, when the hands are at the upper third of the lift. The body may have leaned from its original position, creating a different orbit at the top of the cylinder. The arms may also have moved from the vertical of the imaginary centre, thus imposing the same result as the movement of the body. The illustration above is the result of just such an unconscious movement by either the body or the arms.

Fig 116: Another common problem that affects the making of the cylinder is taking the hands off the clay very quickly. The blue line represents one revolution. When the hands are removed very suddenly, the clay has not completed a revolution. Therefore the clay becomes off centre with this quick release. So *when removing your hands from the clay, do so very gently*, and all the effort of centring will not be in vain. This principle of removing the hands from the clay should be related to every stage of the process, from centring to cutting the form from the wheel head.

Fig 117: This fault is also due to the initial centring procedure. If the centre opening is not continuous from one direction, as in illustration 100, the walls of the cylinder may be thicker on one side than on the other (red arrows). The top edge of the cylinder may also be on an angle, making it very difficult to form a conclusion to the cylinder (yellow line).

Fig 118: These are the basic tools needed for finishing and lifting the cylinder from the wheel head. The base trimmer, shaping rib, wire, and stick sponge are all self-made (though they can easily be bought instead).

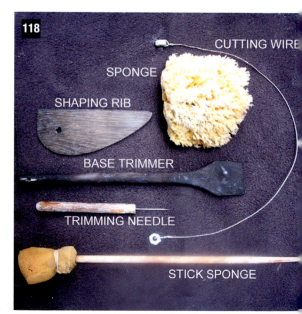

Fig 119: Many tools of special shapes which do specific jobs can be simply made. As mentioned previously, ceramic supply firms also have a wide selection of tools for many applications relating to functional and decorative purposes.

Fig 120: The shaping rib is used to skim over the outside of the cylinder, taking away surface water and slip left over from the third lift.

Fig 121: To lift the form from the wheel head, a twisted wire is needed. If a single strand of wire is used, the form will simply sit down on the flat surface of the wheel head. If the wire is twisted, the form will have a series of grooves, which allow it to be lifted with relative ease.

Making your own twisted wire is very simple. Put the wire around a pencil and secure the pencil at both ends with clay, making sure the wire is as close to the centre of the wheel head as possible.

Fig 122: Hold both ends of the wire and rotate the wheel, though not too fast. A flexible wire about the thickness of 15-amp fuse wire is about right. 15-amp fuse wire is made of copper and is good for smaller forms. Galvanised iron wire of the same thickness can also be used and is much stronger. For easy pulling, use a pair of 6 mm (¼ in) nuts to secure each end of the wire. Ceramic supply companies also have cutting wires, but these are often too tightly wound to give a good release.

enlargement of twisted wire

Fig 123: The wire is used to cut the cylinder from the wheel head.

Fig 124: It is necessary to dry the hands before attempting to lift the cylinder off the wheel.

Fig 125: The dry hands can now lightly grip the cylinder and lift it off the wheel head.

Fig 126: The cylinder can be placed on a ware board made of chipboard or plywood. This should not have been painted or varnished, for fear that the cylinder would stick to a non-absorbent surface.

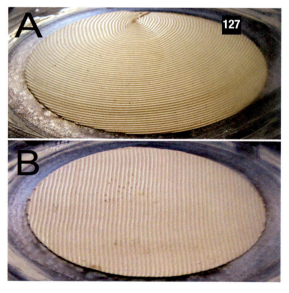

Fig 127: Illustration A shows the pattern of the cutting wire when the wheel head has been rotated slightly as the wire is pulled underneath the cylinder. Illustration B is a straight pull across the wheel head.

As the cylinder was made through the process of rotation, illustration A reflects this process, while illustration B does not. This is just a design consideration, as both methods are equally functional.

Working in series: rhythm and assessment

Fig 128: A sense of rhythm is acquired through repeatedly throwing a simple form. It is important that each piece of clay is the same weight. Repeating the basic cylinder both in width and height as closely as possible is a fundamental exercise for the beginner to practise.

Fig 129: Many of the simple forms that can be made on the wheel will not need additional trimming at a later stage if the initial trimming of the base on the wheel is perfected through practice.

Fig 130: This exercise will establish a confidence in your ability to throw a series of forms that are very closely related to each other. Confidence is necessary to develop and design shapes of personal intent, the subject of the next chapter.

This concludes the basic fundamentals of throwing a cylinder on the potter's wheel. From illustration 58 at the beginning of the previous chapter through to illustration 130 at the end of this one, the relationship between the wheel, the thrower and the clay has been analysed in a logical sequence. It is essential that body and mind develop a sensitivity of touch and physical awareness related to movement. The mechanical principles of the potter's wheel as described in chapter 2 are factual. Psychologically, this is a great advantage. It is totally up to you, the thrower, to understand that when things go wrong, it is not the fault of the wheel or tools used; any adjustments must be made within yourself.

TECHNICAL VOCABULARY AND VISUAL VOCABULARY:
THE INSEPARABLE LANGUAGE OF DESIGN

This chapter is based on the assumption that the reader of this book has practised and developed their technique until they are able to throw a cylinder to a reasonable standard. The reader will thus have understood the various principles of throwing on the potter's wheel: *that, during rotation, what happens on one side will happen on the other; that the speed of rotation is related to centrifugal force; the importance of visualising the theoretical centre; and how all these elements are linked to hands, arms, body and movement.* The potter's wheel has been explained by identifying its components and how they work in relation to the movement of the body. An appropriate technical vocabulary has been established with reference to the operation of this mechanical instrument.

Visual vocabulary

Technical competence and knowledge in any medium are never enough to realise visual intention. Technical knowledge responds only to the mechanics of how material and physical relationships function. Although important, this competence will only serve to answer technical questions.

The questions that sustain enthusiasm and prevent boredom over time are:

■ What am I to do? (Intention)

■ How am I to do it? (Selection)

■ Why this way … what if I …? (Critical Assessment)

These critical questions lead to the deeper investigation of personal choice in relation to design.

Three-dimensional design could be defined as an idea realised by assembling materials to communicate the designer's intentions.

It would be a great injustice if the subject of design and the visual vocabulary associated with it was not presented alongside the necessary technical vocabulary. Intention is a conscious consideration applied to the process of selection. Critical assessment can only be realised in relation to a series of forms, based on the same intention, which are assessed when seen side by side. It is through critical assessment that subtle changes are made, not only in developing the form, but also by adding other elements which can enhance personal expression.

Fig 131: This is the standard cylinder that was demonstrated throughout chapter 3. Assuming the beginner has practised throwing a 1 kg (2¼ lb) piece of clay and has acquired a degree of consistency in height and width, the following development will focus on the application of intention, selection and critical assessment. This trio of qualities is the foundation for establishing a visual vocabulary, without which there is little chance of going beyond technical proficiency.

Fig 132: Illustration 131 is a cylinder without conclusion. Apart from being technically competent, it is void of any intent applied to its form.

To impose a conclusion on the cylinder without changing its basic shape, intention will be first applied to the rim. The compression of the rim has given the form a visual conclusion.

The following series of images will illustrate how to impose variation on the thrown cylinder by selecting and making visual decisions to communicate intention. Remember that all of the following thrown forms begin with a well-centred piece of clay and a cylinder – these *must* be mastered before any attempt can be made to impose other forms that communicate intention.

Fig 133: Selection is introduced as soon as the intention has been established. The above are examples of the selective process applied to the rim. There are two different visual interpretations. In form A the rim is compressed straight across, while form B is compressed on a downward angle. Critical assessment now evaluates how the maker intended these two examples to be visually experienced. Rim A holds the vision directly on top of the form while rim B directs the vision to flow downwards, encompassing the entire form from the outside. Both conclusions are valid. It is the maker who communicates to the viewer his / her specific intentions through selection from the various possibilities. It is the maker's responsibility to acquire a visual vocabulary that will give them the capacity to express these intentions.

Fig 134: Form C has a conclusion which directs the vision to the inside, while form D imposes neither an inner nor an outer direction. Form D has a slight outward movement at the top which gives a feeling that the form is being extended upwards.

The maker must realize that they have, through intention and selection, the ability to communicate visual meaning.

Fig 135: In illustration 1 applying a conclusion was not considered in relation to the entire form: the compression of the top was made on a practice cylinder.

In illustration 2 there was a conscious effort to create an upward movement from base to rim. This was done by narrowing the form just above the base. The throwing and narrowing of the base can be seen in the following illustrations.

Fig 136: The first lift is made exactly as in chapter 3, illustrations 95–98. No attempt should be made to narrow the base at this point. This is in order to keep a consistency of wall thickness on the first lift.

After the first lift is made, both hands bring in the bottom of the form as shown above.

Fig 137: The same compression of the base is made after the second lift.
Fig 138: With the base now narrowed, the third lift splays out the form at the conclusion.
Fig 139: Given the narrowness of the bottom, the stick sponge can be used to extract the excess water from inside the form.

Fig 140: The type of conclusion to be made on a particular form is personal to the maker. The four examples shown in illustrations 133 & 134 are very basic. Through critical assessment you will find additional conclusions.

Fig 141: The shaping rib can be used to finalise the form.

Fig 142: The base trimmer is slipped underneath the base without cutting away any clay. It is then slightly lifted to create a lip on the outer edge of the base. This also creates a shadow and visually lifts the form.

Fig 143: Every subtle change to the form extends the visual vocabulary. As in learning any language, whether it be literal, musical or visual, a progressive development is required. It is necessary to develop a form in small degrees, keeping at least one element the same. In the following illustrations the base of the form will stay constant in width and design. The above form visually grows in one movement upwards and outwards from the base without emphasis related to the rim.

Fig 144: The directional change to the upper third of the above form has made a considerable difference in the way it is visually experienced. The upward movement no longer continues outward as in illustration 143. It is not necessary to change a form radically in order to alter what it expresses visually.

Fig 145: In the above illustration the change of direction is developed outwards at its conclusion. It is basically the same form as in illustration 144. At this point of refinement there is no longer any need for water to lubricate the clay; this would only tend to weaken the structure. The hands can be dry and still not stick to the clay as refinement to the form is considered.

Fig 146: The development of the form can continue until the maker is satisfied with the relationship of base, middle and conclusion.

Fig 147: The above form is divided into three segments of alternately concave and convex structure. These three areas are infinitely variable in their proportion to each other. Working in series with a simple form will not only create variety, but will also add to the visual vocabulary.

Fig 148: The shaping rib tool can also be used to draw lines on the surface of the form.

Fig 149: Comparing illustration 147 with this illustration, the vision no longer flows without interruption. The line drawn at the transitional point between concave and convex has given the form a feeling of a lower portion and an upper portion divided by the change in visual direction.

Fig 150: Placing the line in the centre of the convex portion of the form and slightly higher than centre from the base has given both sections, divided by the line, equal visual importance. If the intention is to do exactly what is illustrated above, the line becomes a valid statement. If the line was put there for its own sake, it does not communicate to the viewer the specific intention of the maker. Placement is paramount.

Fig 151: With the introduction of two lines the placement becomes very critical. A drawn line on a form is a conscious visual statement placed to draw the viewer's attention. These marks should not be arbitrary and repetitive, as this would diminish the impact of the visual statement.

Fig 152: The drawn line at the base of this form adds to visual stability, as the vision is held for a second before moving up the form to settle on another line where the form opens outward to its conclusion. The lines act as visual pauses, like commas in a sentence.

The variations in the last five examples have been relatively subtle, using line to express differences in visual expression.

Fig 153: The upper half has a greater opening and lifting feeling in springing from the lower half of the form, where the drawn line emphasises the change in visual direction. Throwing has this unique ability to make marks which are clearly associated with rotation. The lower half clearly shows these throwing marks. It is up to the maker to recognise when these marks are valid and can add another dimension to the form.

Fig 154: The visual focus is on the central portion of this form. The expansion of this section is what gives it its dominant feature. There is also an interesting relationship between the line drawn on the inside of the rim and the one drawn on the outside at the point of directional change.

Fig 155: The throwing rings have a strong horizontal visual direction around the middle of this form, which is also echoed by the quick outward turn of the conclusion.

Fig 156: This form was considered to be a development of the same basic cylinder featured since the beginning of this chapter. The subtle difference in this case is in how this form springs directly from the base without the change in direction that was a characteristic of all previous illustrations. The narrowness of the base visually lifts the form.

Fig 157: Any changes are considered, in small degrees, following assessment of the previous form. By working this way design and skills can be explored together. Radical changes for their own sake can be detrimental to development. Note how the weight of this form has been shifted downwards, while the neck has been extended, helping visual lift.

Figs 158–163: Working in series helps to develop the skill of throwing a spherical form. The body of all six forms stays more or less the same so as to enable the exploration of a variety of different conclusions. This gives each its own individuality. The six forms represent a progression of study and a visual record of changes imposed on what is basically the same form.

Fig 164: In making a spherical form the procedure of narrowing the base is the same as in illustration 136.

Fig 165: After the second lift the base is again taken in – how much is easily observed by looking at the bottom of the form from inside.

Fig 166: The base will be naturally slightly thicker in wall section because of the base being taken in. This thickness will give the outward development of the form more stability. Starting from the base, the movement is outwards and upwards.

Fig 167: When the lift is three quarters of the way up, ease off and let the outside hand ride over the inside hand, leaving the top narrower than the middle portion. This was the third lift of the clay.

Fig 168: The development of the spherical shape continues from the bottom. The shaping rib can be used to take in the bottom of the form by pushing the tip inwards (red arrow). The body is now pushed outwards from the inside against the rib. From this point onwards, water to lubricate the development is no longer needed.

Fig 169: The form is continually being supported by the inside hand, not only pushing outwards against the rib, but also lifting upwards as the movement changes direction towards the conclusion. Without the use of water, the clay is being pushed together, giving additional structural strength.

Fig 170: Turning the form inwards can be a slight problem. In considering the conclusion, it helps to support the form from the inside. The fingers lift upwards while the rib pushes downwards. The rib should be directly pushing on the finger (red line).

Fig 171: When the opening of the form cannot accommodate the fingers, it is possible to work the rib against the sponge stick.

Fig 172: Finishing the base of the form can be done by assessing the narrowness of the base in relation to the volume, and how visually you intend the form to be presented to the viewer. This always has to be the maker's ultimate consideration. If the form is less than you intended because technically something has gone wrong, or it lacks a quality that has been achieved before, *destroy it*. A compromise at this stage would be an injustice to the development of the visual language of both the viewer and the maker.

Fig 173: The conclusion to the form can now be considered.

Fig 174: When an extension to the spherical body of the form is intended, the upper third should be developed vertically, giving plenty of clay to be taken in (red lines).

Fig 175: The opportunity to expand the body must be done before attempting to close the form, remembering the inside hand is continually in support.

Fig 176: Closing the form is always difficult for beginners. The maker is continually working against centrifugal force, which tends to throw the clay outwards. It is very easy to open a form outwards and very difficult to close it inwards. To relieve the effect of centrifugal force, keep the speed of revolutions as low as possible when bringing in the neck.

Fig 177: The feeling of lifting the clay is very important. With a spherical form, if the pressure is downward to any degree, the form tends to collapse. Sensitivity of feel is truly put to the test when the maker's intention is to produce this particular form.

Fig 178: The feel of centring is most critical right at the very beginning when the clay is first opened to be raised. If the clay is slightly off centre this will be reflected in the final stages. As the form is developed an experienced thrower will be able to compensate for many things and still succeed, but the beginner cannot do this. When the centring is right it will be felt. This feeling cannot be described: the only way to understand it is through dedicated practice.

Fig 179: If the form comes close to the maker's intention another element, such as a line, may be considered. It should be made as a visual enhancement, rather than a random addition.

Fig 180: In the spherical form the visual lift from the base is of prime importance. This is why the diameter of the base is so closely considered. A very personal decision, this can only be evaluated through the maker's own selective process applied to critical assessment. This can be done by placing a series of the same intended forms side by side and observing the relationship of the base to the volume of the spherical shape.

Fig 181: The wide base can also be thought of in terms of the cylindrical family. The previous forms tended to evolve from a narrow base. While visually lifting the form, this can give the feeling of instability. The wide-base form on the other hand gives the impression of being very stable indeed.

A wide base or a narrow one should be considered as elements within the visual vocabulary applied to the selective process.

Fig 182: It is very difficult to assess form when sitting above the work. A mirror is of great assistance in evaluating structure. The maker can see the shape clearly and make adjustments without the need to dismount for further assessment.

Fig 183: *How* to make the form cannot be separated from *why* the form has taken that particular shape. When it is known *how*, then the maker can apply, investigate and develop *why*.

184

185

Figs 184 & 185: These Illustrations represent the throwing movements applied to the basic cylinder. From the moment *how* is mastered (which with dedication to technique can be quite quickly), it is *why* which sustains continual development of visual ideas.

The cylinder is the mother of her six children. The cylinder is without character. It does not imply individualism. The six have their own individual shape, even though they started out as the form of the mother cylinder. From these basic six, a family of thousands could be conceived.

Fig 186: CYLINDER **Fig 187: SPHERE** **Fig 188: CONE**

Illustrations 186–188 represent the three principal shapes which can be made on the potter's wheel. They are non-representational and can therefore be referred to as being *abstract*.

Figs 189, 190 & 191: 189–191 are basically the very same as illustrations 186–188, except they are now presented as hollow forms which can be seen to be derived from the cylinder, sphere and cone. They can now have a dual identity as both an abstract shape and a pot or vessel.

Figs 192, 193 & 194: To contemplate changes of proportion within a series (illustrations 192–194) the maker would have to see the form as a combination of abstract shapes (cylinder and cone) and not merely as a pot or vessel. Therefore critical assessment would use abstract analysis to contemplate these changes.

Fig 195: In this illustration the sphere dominates visually only in relation to the size of the cone. The maker has to evaluate the differences between the two forms. This is best done through a series of the same two forms in varying proportions to each other.

Fig 196: The transformation of cylinder to cone is very subtle. Nevertheless, the maker can still perceive the transitional point from which the cone is developed outwards from the cylinder. The maker's intention is what governs how the form is to be presented to the viewer.

Fig 197: All three elements – the cylinder, sphere and cone – are present in this form. They are purposely assembled without subtlety in order that each one can be easily identified. Whether they are subtly or boldly put together, they can be recognised and analysed as basic elements of our three-dimensional world.

So the answers to those questions posed at the beginning of this chapter are as follows:

■ What am I to do? *The intention is to investigate a series of works within a particular idea.*

■ How am I to do it? *Select a form or combination of forms to be used in the series.*

■ Why this way … what if I …? *Apply abstract analysis for critical assessment of the series.*

Intention, selection, critical assessment and abstract analysis have all been defined. Technical and visual vocabularies in relation to the finished product *cannot* be separated. All of these components are vital not only for the practice and application of the craft of throwing on the potter's wheel, but for all visual work, no matter what the medium may be.

5

THE OPEN FORM

The open form, from the bowl shape to the plate, is basically the outward development of the cylinder. The open form is difficult to lift off the wheel head without it becoming distorted. The solution to this problem is to construct a disc which is placed and secured to the wheel head. This disc acts like a temporary platform for the finished form to sit on while drying, and is easily removed from the wheel without distorting the clay form.

After reading this chapter you will understand how to:

■ make a plaster or plywood disc   63

■ secure the disc to the wheel head   64

■ throw a high and medium open form   65

■ throw a shallow open form   68

■ throw a flat open form   70

■ turn (or trim) the base (all open forms)   71

Making a plaster or plywood disc

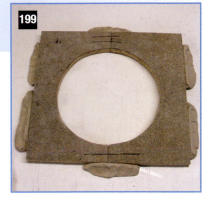

Fig 198: A chipboard former for making a plaster disc can be simply made with a hand jigsaw.

Fig 199: The former for the plaster disc is made of chipboard or any material which is 25 mm (1 in) thick. This thickness is important so that the plaster does not crack. The advantage of plaster is in absorbing moisture from the base of the form being thrown more readily than other materials.

Fig 200: Follow the same procedure as in illustrations 25–36 in chapter 1. The only difference here is that the plaster can be poured all at once because the disc is relatively small (23 cm/9 in) and does not need reinforcement. 1½ to 2 pints of water plus the plaster is sufficient to fill the former.

Securing the disc to the wheel head

Fig 201: With a surf form, round the edges of the cast plaster disc, both top and bottom. Small chips of plaster breaking off the edges and falling into the clay can cause pieces of the thrown clay form to be blown off the surface after it has been fired.

Fig 202: Stiff clay can be used to secure the plaster disc to the wheel head. A plywood disc can be secured in the same way. This is the simplest method for securing the disc when throwing relatively small forms.

Fig 203: Another method of securing the disc to the wheel head is to throw a flat layer of clay 25 mm (1 in) thick – or thicker if many forms are to be thrown in a single session.

Fig 204: Ridges can be put on the layer of clay. This is done if the clay layer is not exactly level.

Fig 205: The plywood disc can also be made with a hand jigsaw as in illustration 198. Dampen the underside and place on the clay, moving it back and forth until it takes hold.

Fig 206: The opening of the clay is very much the same as in illustrations 86 & 87.

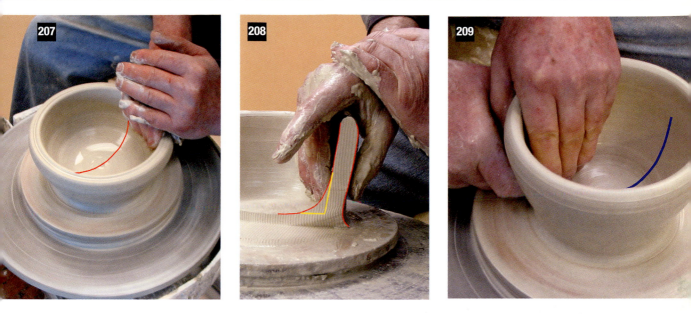

Fig 207: The movement of the right hand is upwards and slightly outwards. The thumb and fingers of the right hand can lift the clay without assistance from the finger of the left hand. This is different from the cylinder, which was slightly wider at the bottom than the top. The development of the open form is just the opposite, being narrower at the bottom and extending outward at the top. The inside of the open form is viewed both from inside and outside. Therefore the curve inside becomes very important. (Left-handed potters should open with their left hand.)

Fig 208: The movement of the left hand follows the red line upwards without creating a right angle (yellow line) as when throwing the cylinder.

Fig 209: The second lift is basically the same as the lift with the cylinder. Special attention is paid to the curve at the base of this open form (blue line).

Fig 210: The third lift is a straight lift concentrating on the diameter of the opening at the top of the form. In the development of the form that follows, the opening at the top will remain pretty much the same diameter.

Fig 211: The inner hand and outer hand work together, developing the body of the form with the shaping rib. At this stage water is not necessary. The pressure from the inside hand against the rib gives strength to the walls of the form.

Fig 212: The base can be trimmed in the same way as the spherical form in illustration 180.

Fig 214: The open form is difficult to lift directly off the wheel head. It is best to let the form stiffen up before lifting it off the plywood disc. Run the cutting wire underneath the disc, leaving the clay slab.

Fig 215: Another plywood disc can immediately be put on the clay, as in illustration 205, ready for the next piece to be thrown.

Fig 213: This cross section clearly shows the flow of the bottom curve (yellow line). The more the form is opened, the more important the curve at the base becomes. The following sequence will focus on this aspect.

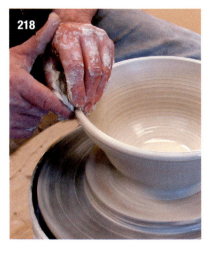

Fig 216: Here the bowl form is being extended outwards at a flatter angle than in illustration 209. The right-hand index finger (yellow line) can be used for support as the clay is lifted (red lines).

Fig 217: The support at the base of the open form is critical. The flatter the bowl form is extended, the further out the base is made when opening the form (red lines).

Fig 218: On the third lift, keep the sides relatively straight while observing the inside of the form.

Fig 219: Without water, the bowl form can now be developed with the shaping rib and the fingers of the inside hand. The shaping rib moves upwards when used on the outside of the form (red arrow) and downwards when used on the inside (see illustration 220).

Fig 220: The right hand (yellow arrow) is in support of the left, which now holds the shaping rib. The continuity of the inside shape can finally be formed by the downward movement of the rib inside the form (red arrow). This is not as easy as it looks, and may have to be repeated several times for the inside curve to look right.

Throwing a shallow open form

Fig 221: When throwing a shallow bowl form, extend the base much further out to create the maximum support for the form. In this situation it is very difficult to judge the thickness of the base, because the thumb of the left hand is quite a distance away from the opening fingers.

Fig 222: Stick the needle tool down through the clay until it hits the plywood disc. Hold the needle and place the index finger on top of the clay. When the needle is withdrawn, the distance between your finger and the end of the needle will indicate the thickness of the base.

Fig 223: If the base is too thick, press down a bit more before opening the clay, and repeat the operation with the needle.

Fig 224: The clay is opened by pulling straight across after the thickness of the base has been established.

Fig 225: It is important that considerable pressure is applied across the base to help prevent cracking during the drying process. Unlike the base, the side walls are continually being pressed together from both sides in the lifting stages of construction. Therefore cracking is extremely rare on the side walls of a form.

Fig 226: The first lift is slightly outwards but mainly vertical, following the same principle as in illustration 207.

Fig 227: The flatter the form, the more attention must be given to the support of the right hand in relation to the left hand.

Fig 228: The shallow form is extended outwards and kept higher than intended.

Fig 229: With continuous support from the right hand, the left hand completes the movement of the rib from the rim to the middle of the form (red arrow) The blue arrow points to where most of the trouble will occur in creating a continuous movement from the rim to the centre. Following the black line, the dip is exactly where the form is no longer supported by the base. Try to keep the right hand supporting the form from underneath the base, as shown in illustration 227.

Throwing a flat open form

Fig 230: For a very flat plate form it is necessary to have a large disc to throw on. This disc can be made of 15 mm (⅝ in) chipboard or plywood.

Fig 231: As mentioned in illustration 225 the base is taken much further out. Compression of the base becomes more critical, so instead of a sponge use the shaping rib, which having a hard edge is more suitable. It is advisable to compress the base two or three times. This will help to prevent cracking of the base during drying.

Fig 232: No matter how far out the base is taken, the first lift is vertical and slightly outwards, as in illustration 226.

Fig 233: The right hand holds the rim firmly while the left hand works with the rib from the rim to the middle of the form, consolidating the base. Note that there are three lugs (yellow arrow) attached to the disc. These go over the edge of the wheel head, preventing the disc shifting from side to side. This is shown again in illustration 234.

Turning (or trimming) the base (all open forms)

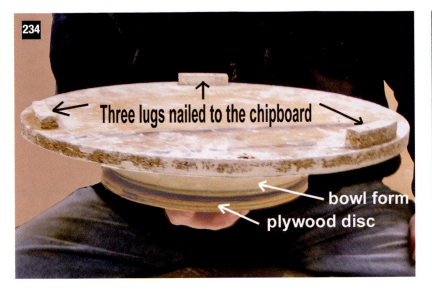

Fig 234: Turning (trimming the base of the form) is required for most open forms. At the turning stage the clay needs to be firm but not completely dried. Any open form is difficult to turn over without putting undue strain on the rim. To avoid this problem a much larger disc can be placed on top of the form.

Fig 235: Placing one hand under and the other hand on top, the shallow form is flipped over. In this way there is no strain on the rim of the form.

Fig 236: With a black marker, centring rings can be drawn on the chipboard disc before the form is placed on top (illustration 234). Without these rings it is difficult to centre the form to be turned. Pieces of clay are placed at the rim in order that it does not move off centre while being turned. The three chipboard lugs go over the rim of the wheel head (yellow lines).

Fig 237: The first consideration is to establish the size of the area to be turned. The method of trimming is the same whether you are right- or left-handed.

Fig 238: There are many different designs of turning tools. This is an apple corer from America. I have used a tool of this design since 1962. Try to avoid taking too great a grip of the clay. It is best to work down to the required thickness in stages.

Fig 239: The condition of the clay when turning is crucial. If the clay is too soft the trimmings will stick to the tool and the pressure may push in the base. Stickiness is related to the softness of the clay. When too hard it will be difficult to get a good grip of the clay. Through a process of trial and error the right condition of hardness will be found.

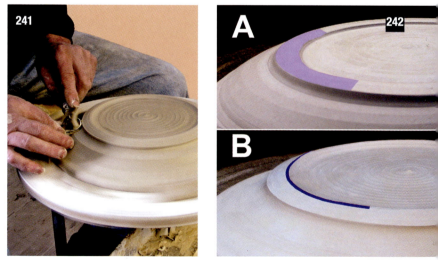

Fig 240: The angle of the foot should be considered in relation to intention. Two options will be discussed in illustration 242 (the red line indicates the angle).

Fig 241: The division between the foot and the body of this shallow form is turned so as to be clearly defined.

Fig 242: In illustration A the base rests on a broad surface being turned straight across, while in illustration B the base rests on a very small area when turned on an angle (illustration 240). Both are technically valid, and the maker can try both options. In this way the maker is adding to both their technical and visual vocabularies, which can then be applied to the selective process.

243

Fig 243: These five illustrations represent a three-dimensional conical form opening in stages towards a relatively flat two-dimensional form. In practising the development of the open form, begin with the vertical and work through to the horizontal as illustrated in the course of this chapter. Successful flat forms are achieved through the careful control of wheel speed, the lack of water after opening the form for the first time, pressure from the hands and other shaping tools, and hand support. Through practice you will develop a feel for these interrelated factors and a sensitivity that will result in the right balance being applied.

chapter

6

THE DISCIPLINE OF FUNCTION

This chapter will present the basic techniques for making functional ware on the potter's wheel.

■ selecting a form to construct a family of functional ware   75

■ pouring lips   76

■ handles   77

■ lids   84

■ galleries   85

■ handles and knobs for lids   86

■ lids with shallow flanges   90

■ lids with deep flanges   92

■ pouring spout   93

■ attaching the spout   95

Selecting a form

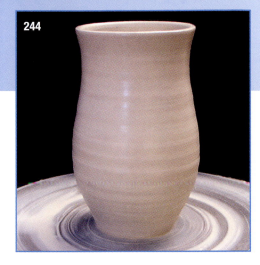

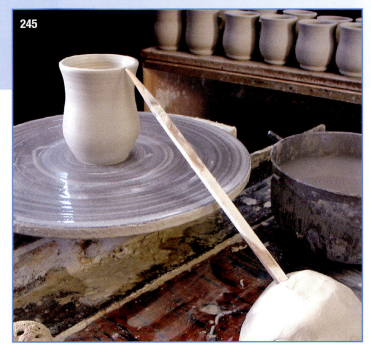

Fig 244: This simple form will be used as the model for creating a series of functional ware, belonging to the same family, beginning with the mug and concluding with the teapot.

Fig 245: The mug is an excellent form to begin with. Creating a series of forms of the same height and rim diameter can be achieved by setting up a pointer. The clay for throwing the mugs must be of a consistent weight. The simple gauge is a pointed piece of wood stuck into a sizeable piece of clay. This method of using a pointer is most useful when there is more than one unit needed. Illustration 294 will show another reason for consistency in height and rim diameter.

Fig 246: In a family of functional ware, it can be desirable to have a base or foot which will adapt to other forms within the set.

Economically it may be impractical to turn over each individual mug for trimming. A profile tool can create a foot without the necessity for trimming.

The profile tool is a piece of 3 mm (⅛ in) thick plastic cut to one's own design. The plastic is very easily cut with a jigsaw or a metal file, and finished with sandpaper.

Fig 247: This profile cutter will be used for all forms of a size related to the mug or slightly bigger. For larger forms within the family, a slightly larger-profile cutter can be made to suit the relationship of foot size to the larger form.

Pouring lips

Fig 248: The jug or pitcher is a single unit within the family and therefore a pointer is not necessary. The consistency of height will be in relation to the weight of clay. Pouring lips will vary to a degree, making the rim diameter not so critical.

The fingers indicated by the green arrows keep the rim from being pulled out as the finger of the other hand moves *gently* back and forth, working the rim downwards (red arrow). (A left-hander should work the opposite way, of course.)

Fig 249: The upper fingers (green arrows) pull inwards as the finger of the other hand works back and forth, moving downwards (yellow line). Note the change of finger angle from illustration 248.

Fig 250: The two hands bring the pouring lip together with equal pressure from both sides (green arrows). The inner fingers pull slightly forward as the thumbs push inwards (blue arrows).

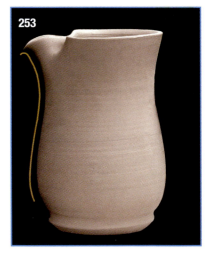

Fig 251: The top fingers pull the lip quite closely together, though not touching (green arrows). The lip is again gently pulled down by the finger moving back and forth in an arching motion (red line).

Fig 252: The reason for pulling the lip so close together, as shown in illustration 251, is that as the jug dries the lip will open. Slightly more opening of the lips can also occur during the glaze firing.

Fig 253: The pulling of the pouring lip should not disturb the profile of the jug. The front profile has remained relatively the same as the back profile.

Handles

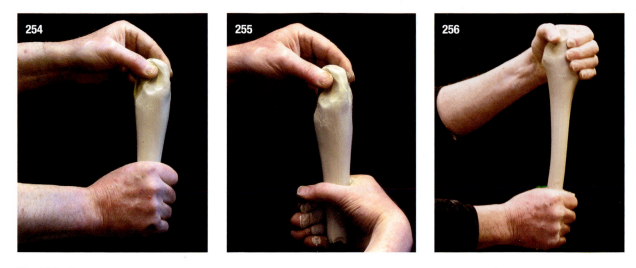

Fig 254: To complete both the mug and the jug, the making of handles is the next priority. Without a mechanical way of making handles, this method of extending a piece of clay into a long strip means it is possible to make four or five handles. Hold a piece of clay in one hand and, with the other hand well lubricated with water, gently extend the clay.
Fig 255: Reverse the lower hand on the next series of downward movements.
Fig 256: Reverse the lower hand again.

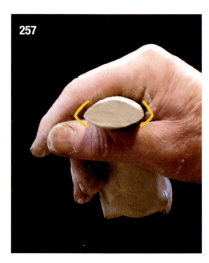

Fig 257: The reason for changing the position of the lower hand when drawing out the clay is to have both sides of the clay symmetrical, not one side pointed and the other side round (yellow markers).

Fig 258: As the clay is drawn down it will become thinner in section though not in width. The width will remain fairly constant as the handle section is continually lengthened.

Fig 259: Remember to keep reversing the lower hand in the lengthening process.

Fig 260: The last operation is to make an indentation down the middle of the drawn section. Thus, when picking up the ware by the handle, the thumb has a very secure place to rest.

Fig 261: The clay handle section can be cut into lengths suitable for handles. This method of drawing a long section from a piece of clay will take considerable practice. Another factor is the plasticity of the clay. If the clay tears off in the lengthening process, it may be what is termed as being *short* (i.e. not plastic).

Extruded handles

Fig 262: The mechanical way of making handles is to make a profile of a handle design with a piece of plastic which is 6 mm (¼ in) thick. This thickness is necessary to prevent the plastic cracking under the pressure of clay being pushed against it. Drill a couple of holes near the centre and with a black marker draw the design.

Fig 263: The plastic will cut very easily with a jigsaw or band saw and will also file very easily. Plastic is a softer material than brass or aluminium and will wear much more quickly, especially if the clay has sand or grog in it. But for trial purposes, the plastic is ideal until the design is well established. Using steel for the template is not a good idea: rust is difficult to clean and could easily contaminate white clay bodies.

Fig 264: This is a manual extruding machine. The template is placed in the base ring and secured to the base of the cylindrical pipe by clips.

Fig 265: The cylindrical pipe is filled with clay and the handle is pulled down. This pushes the clay through the handle profile, and lengths of clay are extruded. These machines are very reasonable in price compared with a de-airing pug. There are many other extruding possibilities besides handle-making, and as such a machine like this one is a very worthwhile investment for your own studio.

Fig 266: A de-airing pug has the advantage of being more continuous when extruding lengths of clay to be used for handles. Also, being de-aired adds considerably to the plasticity of the clay, eliminating cracking when handles are curved into a tight radius.

Fig 267: The length of clay for each article will vary. A board marked out with lines for a particular article will save a great deal of time.

Fig 268: It is an advantage to work as close to eye level as possible, whether standing or seated.

Fig 269: Dampen the area where the handle is to be placed. Whether or not the handles crack at the points where they are attached to the ware will depend to a great extent on the quality of the clay and the drying conditions. Thus the condition of the ware, whether too dry or too soft, will need to be evaluated. If only one handle out of 20 cracks there may not be a problem; if 15 crack then there is definitely a problem to be sorted out.

Fig 270: Hold the handle vertically and attach the clay with a diagonal, 45-degree movement of the thumb.

The handle should look as if it is growing out of the body, and not merely attached to it.

Fig 271: The movement on the opposite side is exactly the same.

Fig 272: Care must be taken not to bend the handle too quickly. From the place where it is attached to the body, keep the visual flow moving upwards with a generous loop, as indicated by the red line.

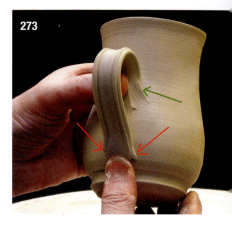

Fig 273: A thumb print at the base of the ware will be sufficient to secure the handle at the base. The outer edges of the handle at the base (red arrows) are finished in exactly the same way as the attachments at the upper part of the handle (green arrow).

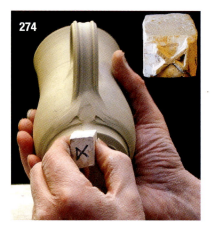

Fig 274: A stamp to identify the maker is a very quick way of signing the ware and can easily be made with a piece of plaster. When the ware is much larger and more individual, a signature and date may be more appropriate.

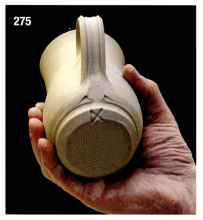

Fig 275: The finished article is left to dry until ready to be processed through the finishing cycle.

Fig 276: The next handle is pulled directly on the form. The places where the piece of clay is to be attached need to be well secured. It is helpful to score the ware at the point of attachment before dampening it with a sponge.

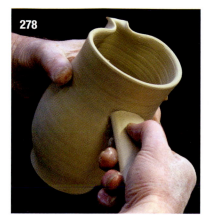

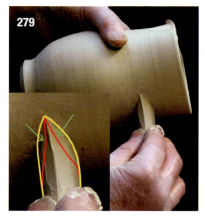

Fig 277: Follow the same procedure as in illustrations 254 and 255. Only a short piece is needed, quite thick in section.

Fig 278: The clay section is firmly attached to the body of the ware by pushing gently at the position which was scored in illustration 276.

Fig 279: The hand pushes the clay from above and underneath, creating a knife-edge. This happens equally on both sides. There is a danger that too much pressure is exerted when pushing the piece of clay onto the body. The red line and the green arrows indicate where this is likely to happen. The yellow lines are how the form of the attachment should look before the clay is lengthened to form the handle.

Fig 280: This again is exactly the same as in illustrations 254 and 255.

Fig 281: The thumb creates an indentation down the middle of the handle in the same way as in illustration 260.

Fig 282: If the clay has not been pushed excessively at the point where it was put onto the body, the handle should support itself and make a well-formed curve.

Fig 283: As the handle is secured at the base of the ware, the excess clay from the pulling process will simply come away.

Fig 284: A final impression with the index finger will complete the handle.

Fig 285: After securing the handle at the base, a small adjustment may be necessary to the upper part of the handle by putting the index finger underneath and lifting slightly (green arrow). The red line shows how the handle springs upwards from the body. If the handle came straight out, it would give the impression of drooping.

Slab handles

Fig 286: This is the simplest way of making a handle without the use of an extruding machine. The pulling methods, illustrations 254–260 and illustrations 277–285, take considerable practice.

With a rolling pin and a couple of strips of wood of equal thickness it is relatively easy to make a slab of clay.

Fig 287: Deciding on the width of the handle, a stick can serve to cut a number of clay strips.

Fig 288: The clay-strip edges are sponged down and rounded with a sponge.

Fig 289: After sponging restore the two strips of wood that were used to create the thickness of the slab of rolled-out clay (illustration 286). This will prevent the clay being pushed outwards when making the impression of the lines on the strip of clay, and it will also keep the clay strip straight.

Fig 290: The lines on the strip of clay are made with a piece of wood tapered to a sharp edge. The advantage of making handles with this technique is that the impressed lines can vary in design (illustration 292).

Fig 291: The strips of clay can be cut into lengths and applied to the ware as handles in the same way as with the drawn or extruded handles.

Fig 292: These are a few of the variations in design made by impressing the tapered piece of wood onto the length of clay (illustration 290). Extrusions as well as pulling of the handle will not give these variations as easily.

Fig 293: These are two examples of the application of handles which has been discussed in this chapter. It is important to be functional: the ware should feel comfortable and secure when lifted by their handles.

Fig 294: In illustration 245, it was mentioned that there is more than one reason for throwing mugs and soup bowls to a pointer. In a bisque firing (firing of the ware before glazing) it is possible to load the kiln without the use of shelves. This is possible if the rims are close enough in diameter to stack one on top of the other.

Fig 295: At the beginning of this chapter a pouring lip and handles were applied to the cylindrical form, creating the jug and mug. The rest of the chapter will develop a series derived from the open form of the soup bowl. The similar profile of the jug and the soup bowl is what conveys a family likeness (green lines).

Lids

Fig 296: The bodies of the jam and sugar pot are much the same as the soup bowl in both form and size. The lid is relatively small and is thus better made from a large piece of clay, which will also be enough to throw the body of the pot. This is known as 'throwing off the hump'. After centring, squeeze enough clay to form the lid from the top of the main piece of clay.

Fig 297: The right hand can easily work from underneath, supporting the clay while the left hand opens the shallow lid. Because of the small size of this lid it would be more difficult working directly on the wheel head.

Fig 298: Extend the clay outwards until the desired size is established.

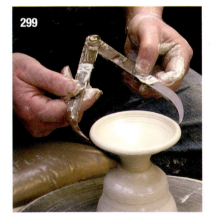

Fig 299: A pair of callipers is used to measure the outside size.

Fig 300: Cut off the lid with the twisted wire. Working higher it is very easy to lift the lid off the larger piece of clay.

Fig 301: Remove the lid and set aside to firm up before trimming.

Fig 302: A second pair of callipers is used to record the measurement to be used as the inside diameter of the body.

Fig 303: The body of the pot is made from the remainder of the clay after the lid has been removed. The top rim is left quite thick to accommodate what is known as the gallery.

Fig 304: The gallery is made after the first lift by pressing down about half the thickness of the rim with the thumb of the left hand. This is so that the wall of the body still has the strength to support the downward pressure.

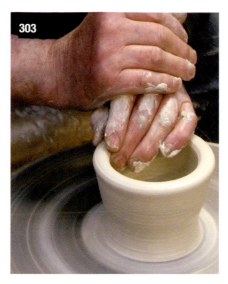

Fig 305: The body can now be developed without fear of the form collapsing.
Fig 306: The inside callipers check that the lid will fit. The form is still flexible enough to allow an adjustment to be made by either pushing the rim inward or pulling it outward.

Handles and knobs for lids

Fig 307: When the clay is ready for trimming, secure the lid to the wheel head with stiff clay so that the lid does not shift its central position. If there is a danger of too much pressure when trimming, place a small piece of stiff clay underneath before putting the lid on the wheel head. The larger the lid the more danger there is that the middle will sink.

Fig 308: The excess clay is trimmed off, leaving a well-structured dome-like form.

Fig 309: The centre is scored and dampened, and a small ball of clay is separately formed as a thrown knob handle.

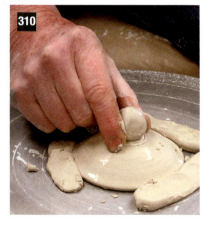

Fig 310: The small piece of clay is placed in the centre.

Fig 311: The knob is centred and thrown.

Fig 312: The handle should visually communicate security of handling and be in proportion to the combination of lid and body.

Fig 313: Except for the different type of handle, the process for finishing this lid is exactly the same as that for the previous lid.

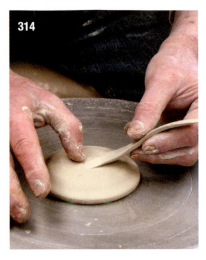

Fig 314: This is similar to how the handles were put on mugs and jugs. The handle is pulled and the selected section is applied.

Fig 315: All methods are carried forward to new applications. These methods are part of the growing selective vocabulary.

Fig 316: In making this lid the knob is formed first. The thumb of either hand runs downwards, creating a small conical shape.

Fig 317: When the proportion of this conical shape is considered to be right, the thumb of either hand pushes inwards, creating a stem.

Fig 318: When this is created the fingers push from underneath, leaving a ring of clay below the unfinished knob.

Fig 319: This ring of clay can now be thrown outwards.

Fig 320: The rim is extended outwards.

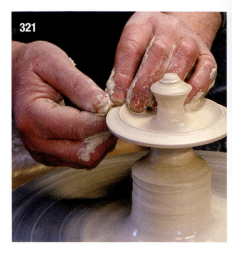

Fig 321: Flatten the outer edge, which will sit into the gallery of the body.

Fig 322: The knob is finished and the proportions and security of handling considered.

Fig 323: The lid is cut off with a twisted wire as in illustration 300 and set aside.

Fig 324: The body is exactly the same as in illustration 305. Do not let the newly thrown lid touch the body at this stage while still wet. Once it has firmed up, the lid can be lifted and assessed for being the right size for the body, which itself can be adjusted, if necessary, as in illustration 306.

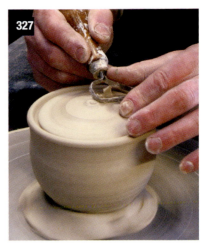

Fig 325: The base of the body can be trimmed as required.

Fig 326: When both the lid and the body are leatherhard, the body can be used as a chuck for trimming the lid.

Fig 327: The underside of the lid is trimmed to remove the excess clay.

Fig 328: The trimming tool can also serve as a cutter to allow space for a spoon.

Fig 329: These are the three finished pots. The bodies are all the same, with only variations in the lids.

Lid with shallow flange

Fig 330: A larger lid can be made with the same technique used for the smaller lids for the sugar and jam pots. This lid is being made for a storage jar.

Fig 331: The larger the lid, the broader the base left underneath (green line). As the lid is opened out, the rim is left thick for an upstand flange to be made. The red line shows the slight indication of this flange.

Fig 332: The right index finger pushes downwards, creating the flange.

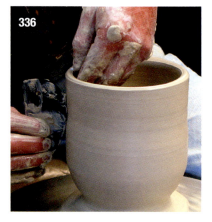

Fig 333: A pair of callipers is used to measure the outside diameter of the flange.

Fig 334: The lid is set aside for drying to leatherhard. The lid will then be turned over, trimmed, and the handle put on.

Fig 335: The remaining clay can be thrown for the body of the storage jar.

Fig 336: The body of the storage jar is thrown without a gallery in the rim.

Fig 337: In illustration 333 the callipers measured the outside diameter of the flange. A second pair of calipers check that the inside diameter of the storage jar will let the flange of the lid drop inside (illustration 341).

Fig 338: When the lid is leatherhard, it is trimmed ready for the handle to be applied.

Fig 339: A handle is pulled in the same way as for the mugs and jugs.

Fig 340: Instead of looping the handle as in illustration 315, both ends are attached separately.

Fig 341: The storage jar is now complete, with the flange preventing the lid from slipping off.

Lid with deep flange

Fig 342: The lids for teapots are different from the lids demonstrated so far. This lid starts out exactly like the lid in illustration 319. But considerably more clay is allowed for the lifting of the flange.

Fig 343: The deep flange is created and the outer edge turned outwards so that the lid does not fall into the teapot. (The teapot is made without a gallery, as in the casserole.) In addition, the deep flange does not allow the lid to drop out of the teapot when it is tilted and poured.

Fig 344: Pressure is applied to the stem of the lifting knob, to bring it higher up for easier handling of the lid. For trimming the base of the lid follow illustrations 326 and 327.

Fig 345: Another type of teapot lid starts out identical to the lid for the cover jar (illustration 331).

Fig 346: The flange is lifted upwards. It is high for the reason given in illustration 343 (above).

Fig 347: Both types of teapot lid are squeezed from underneath and cut off with a twisted wire (illustration 300). They are set aside to firm up for trimming. Follow Illustrations 310 to 312 for throwing the knob for the second type of lid.

Pouring spout

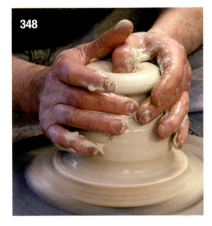

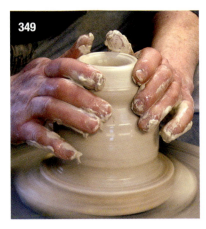

Fig 348: Making a pouring spout for a teapot is based on the form of the cylinder. Lids are related to the open form. The basic principles of throwing either form apply. Both items are quicker and easier thrown off the hump.

Fig 349: Once thrown, the spout will be set aside until firm enough to be applied to the body of the teapot.

Fig 350: From a small indentation just below the base of the spout (green arrow) a conical cylinder is formed.

Fig 351: The forming of the spout is very similar to the forming of the neck (see chapter 3, illustrations 176– 178).

Fig 352: The clay is slowly brought up and inwards.

Fig 353: The spout is still short enough that the middle finger is able to reach the base, which is now given a convex shape (green line). The top is continued upwards in the form of a narrow cylinder (yellow line).

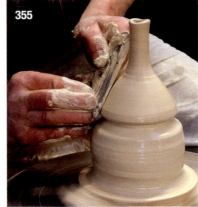

Fig 354: The upper part of the spout is refined and drawn into a narrow and thin-walled cylinder. The spout is brought up higher than may eventually be necessary, because later it will be cut to its final shape after being applied to the body of the teapot (illustration 368).

Fig 355: The rib finishes the form and removes excess water from the surface of the clay.

Fig 356: A needle cuts off the spout at its base (red arrow).

Fig 357: The spout is lifted off and left to stiffen.

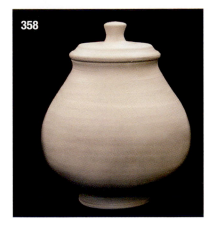

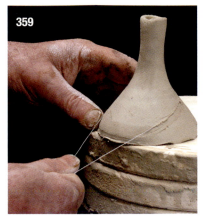

Fig 358: The body of the teapot at this stage is the same as a cover jar except for the deep flange of the lid. In profile this cover jar still relates to the family of ware.

Fig 359: The spout, when firm, is ready to be applied to the body. With a fine *untwisted* wire, the base of the spout is cut at an angle. The wire is looped around the spout and pulled downwards.

Fig 360: The bottom part is discarded.

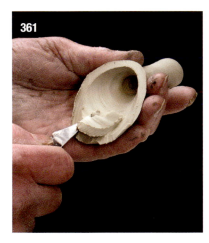

Fig 361: The inside edge is trimmed in order to blend into the round body of the teapot.

Fig 362: A line is drawn on the body to indicate the positioning of the spout. Bear in mind that the body will ultimately be filled with liquid, so pay special attention to the angle and height of the spout in relation to the body. Follow illustration 367.

Fig 363: The strainer holes should be at the upper part of the spout, and large enough to allow a good quantity of liquid to pass through. A nice pattern is also desirable. The holes can be made with a hole-maker or drill bit. Twist your tool as it is going through the wall of the body. This will prevent the clay between the holes from breaking.

Fig 364: Score the outer edge where the spout will be connected.

Fig 365: Dampen both the scored edge on the body and the spout.

Fig 366: The spout is placed on the body following the scored edge.

Fig 367: This side view shows the relationship of the spout to the top rim of the teapot body. If lower than the broken yellow line the liquid will pour out even before the tea is poured. The spout is sponged around its edge to secure a good bond between the two parts.

Fig 368: The untwisted wire is placed around the end of the spout and cut level with the top edge of the body.

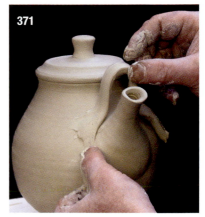

Fig 369: The pouring edge of the spout can be slightly worked over in the same way as was done with the jug (illustration 251).

Fig 370: The angle of the spout may seem peculiar, but is needed because the spout will twist in the glaze firing. The exact angle to be cut will depend on the type of clay and the temperature of the glaze firing. Because the wheel is revolving anticlockwise, the angle will always be cut as shown.

Fig 371: The balance of a teapot for easy pouring is an important consideration. A teapot once filled with liquid becomes considerably heavier no matter what size it may be. Conventional approaches tend to be the single back handle or overhead handle. But a teapot of this type can take considerable wrist strength to pour. A handle in the front and a handle in the rear is a practical solution to the problem.

Fig 372: The back handle is applied to the body in the same way as the front handle. It is placed lower in the back for better leverage when pouring.

Fig 373: The teapot, which is derived from the cover jar, represents in a single item the use of all the components described within this chapter.

Fig 374: Just as the mug, jug, cover jar and teapot are all related to the cylinder, so the other members of the family are related to the open form. The casserole is a high-sided open form. The lid is a shallow open form, turned over to be trimmed, and a knob then placed on top for the casserole lid.

Fig 375: The serving bowl is derived from a lower open form, and the dinner plate is a flat open form. The cheese or butter dish is a combination of these two forms, with the serving bowl turned upside down, trimmed, and a knob thrown on top.

Fig 376: More items could be included in this family of functional ware: side plates, cups and saucers, dessert bowls, gravy servers, etc. These items represent variations of scale and visual relationship to the basic family shape. No attempt was made to personalise the forms. Designing the visual and functional relationships of the items to each other was the principle exercise. Chapters 4, 5 and 6 contain the entire range of technical vocabulary necessary to build a personal identity in ceramics, based either on functional ware or on one-off individual pieces.

The practice and experience of making an entire family of functional ware (illustration 376) is a significant and far-reaching exercise. It is a confidence-building process in understanding relationships of scale and form, and the functional tactility of knobs and handles, of lids which fit properly, and lips and spouts which pour easily and relate visually to the form.

The balance between technical skill and personal expression must eventually become inseparable, so that the work can flow directly from your personal intention. The maker cannot do this through technique alone. Technique and individuality are harmonised through intention, selection and critical assessment.

Questions relating to *how* refer to tangible techniques to be practised repeatedly until skill and knowledge become integral responses to material and tools. However, skill and knowledge alone do not make great ceramics. There need to be 'additional tangibles' that relate to the critical question of *why*. The visual vocabulary; intention, selection and critical assessment – these are what will eventually make the work unique and identifiable as your own. Chapter 7 will examine this process more thoroughly.

7 RUDIMENTS OF EXPRESSION

This chapter introduces visual elements that can be applied by the designer as part of a repertoire of personal expression. Clay is the medium here, refined and formed either with or without the potter's wheel.

The visual elements are synonymous with developing your visual vocabulary and should be deeply and consciously considered at every stage of the creative process.

The nine visual elements are *line*, *shape*, *tone*, *colour*, *texture*, *form*, *scale*, *space* and *light*. These nine elements are not abstract. They are real, visible and tangible. The maker's awareness of them is an integral component of the making process.

■ identifying the nine elements   101

■ visual elements in two-dimensional design   104

■ textures   107

Identifying the nine elements in our visual world

Fig 377: The tendency when looking at objects is to identify them by name, e.g. the branches of a tree. But the branches can also be interpreted as *line*. The left-hand image is a strong vertical line accompanied by lines on either side giving an outward and upward movement. The right-hand image is a series of vertical and diagonal lines. The smaller and lighter lines tie the heavier lines together.

All the nine elements in our visual world will be analysed in the above manner, and their application defined, later in this chapter. This process is known as abstract analysis.

Fig 378: As with the abstract analysis of the branches in illustration 377, it is not difficult to define the contrasting *shapes* in the above images. The stone wall on the left is made up of a series of large and small shapes with a very irregular pattern: a visual variety of texture and colour is experienced on the surface of the stone. When looking at and applying an analytical appraisal to our visual world, combinations of elements are inevitable. The brick wall, because of its factory-made shape and texture might be visually less exciting. Nevertheless, for expressive reasons, the brick could fit an intended purpose by lending a modular motif to the work.

Fig 379: This winter scene communicates a cold and rather austere environment. The snow-covered field and the sky are very close in *tone*. This adds to a sombre feeling. Space and scale play a significant role in this scene. These additional visual elements create the distance when set against the small scale of the building on the horizon in relation to the position of the viewer. The distance between the viewpoint and the building will always be determined by the visual scale of that building. Within the compositional framework of this scene, the ploughed, snow-covered field also has a linear visual direction ending at the horizon.

Fig 380: *Colour* is the most influential of the nine elements. The awareness of colour plays a significant part in everyone's visual world. Colour is the one element where choice is exercised in a very personal way almost every day through the apparel we choose to wear and the selection of decor within the home and workplace.

The range of colour is limitless and thus colour is capable of creating an immense variety of moods and visual intensities. Differences in tone and the relationships between different colours and textures are the most influential factors within design decision-making.

Fig 381: These are just a few examples of *texture* in nature. This can be visually understood without the necessity of touch. Nevertheless, texture is part of our tactile world and is experienced every day through touch when picking up a bath towel or a scrubbing pad at the sink.

The conscious application of texture in the making process has, like colour, an almost limitless range of visual and actual feel between extremes of smooth and rough.

Texture applied to ceramics is extremely easy because the material is soft. Even when dry, before firing, texture is easily applied to ceramic. It is for this reason that the way the selective process is applied is so important.

Fig 382: When experiencing *form*, it would be valuable to look at the structure in geometric terms, in order that the proportion of the parts to each other can be appraised. For instance, consider the relationship between the rectangular shape and the cylindrical shape it sits atop at the corner of the building. Also, observe the window openings and their placement relative to each other within the overall structure.

Drawing is the best way to assess your ability to record these proportional relationships. It is only when you can demonstrate to yourself that the drawing expresses these proportional relationships accurately that it would then be valid to do the exact opposite through intention. Example: Picasso's earliest work as opposed to his later work.

Fig 383: *Scale* and *space* are closely related. The image on the left illustrates the difference between the larger rough-textured boulder and the smaller rock with a smooth surface. The relationship in terms of scale to each other, the dissimilarity between the two, is accentuated when they are close together. The recognition of space, as seen in the second image, relates to the distance between objects and our knowledge of their actual size: the ceramic sculpture on the rock is 60 cm (24 in) in height, while the height of the Bass Rock, lying one mile off the north-east coast of Scotland, near the township of North Berwick, is 100 m (313 ft).

Fig 384: *Light* has a profound effect on all that is seen. The atmosphere which light can create is relevant to all nine elements, whether this is created artificially through electricity, which can be relatively constant, or by natural daylight, which is constantly changing. Either source of light has a dramatic effect on our visual world.

Figs 377–384: These images are nine illustrations of natural reality. The various elements have been examined through abstract analysis in order that they will be recognised when making visual observation and assessment for design reasons. To build a design vocabulary, it is necessary to go beyond recognising line, shape, colour, tone and texture within the context of realism. It is essential to examine the elements individually and in conjunction with each other in a purely abstract arrangement.

The following examination of the elements will be presented two-dimensionally on a shallow thrown form. At the conclusion of this chapter, a series of finished works will be used to identify the abstract qualities in the same manner as they were analysed in illustrations 377–384.

Line

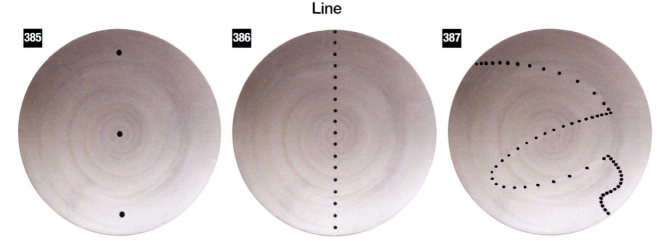

Fig 385: Communicating visual meaning is about placement of visual marks and how these marks are interpreted by the viewer.

In illustration 385 the three marks can be seen as being *in line* (rather than as a line) because of the large spacing between the marks. Nevertheless, intentionally, the dots communicate their central and vertical position in relation to the circular shape.

Fig 386: These marks are in exactly the same position in relation to the circular shape as those in illustration 385. By filling in the spaces with additional marks, a visual line has been created. This may not provoke a great deal of visual response from the viewer because of its diagrammatic formality.

Fig 387: The placement of these marks, in relation to illustration 386, has variety not only in the spaces between the marks, but also in the change of directional movement, adding a considerable amount of interest to the dotted line.

Line and accent

Fig 388: These are two contrasting lines. The horizontal line gives the impression of flowing without interruption, while the vertical line is ridged and angular. The lines being the same thickness only emphasises their visual differences. This would be the case no matter where they were placed in relation to each other.

Fig 389: Although within the same format as illustration 388, the placement of an accent on the flowing line by thickening a portion directs the eye to this accent.

The maker must realise they are fully in command of how to steer the viewer's vision.

Fig 390: This illustration demonstrates that even though the format may change in relation to the two contrasting lines, the accents and their placement steer the vision in opposite directions.

Shape

Fig 391: The original format of illustration 388 will be used to demonstrate working in series. Changes and effects can easily be identified from one image to the next. A shape is added to the vertical line and placed in a position that integrates it with the line. A dark-grey colour has been chosen for this shape so as not to dominate the black accent.

Fig 392: The triangular shape is moved diagonally across to the opposite side of the vertical line. A relationship remains between the line and the shape because the triangular shape in the vertical figuration was not positioned lower or higher than the diagonal line.

Fig 393: In illustrations 391 and 392 reference was made to a relationship between the shape and the line. In this illustration, the circle is a contrasting element even though the scale and the position of the circle are relatively the same. The accent on the flowing line has the same value as the circle, giving the image a greater unity.

Line, shape and colour

Shape and colour

Tone

Fig 394: The choice of colour and accent can change the visual appearance considerably, even though the format remains unchanged, as in illustrations 391–393. Note how the yellow shape is far less dominant because of its tonal similarity to the background. Another accent in blue has been placed on the vertical line, which acts as a countermovement to the red accent on the flowing line.

Fig 395: In illustration 394, the lines and the triangular shape are drawn onto the grey background. When the shapes around the lines are filled in with different colours, they are seen as shapes of red, green, yellow and orange. The accent on the flowing line is blue and has its own identity as a shape, while the blue triangular shape remains independent against the red background.

Fig 396: Tone has the ability to harmonise the image. Tonal values, no matter whether they are dark or light, always have this unifying capability as long as all the tonal values remain the same.

Simulated and photographic textures

1

2

Actual texture

3

Fig 397: Primarily, there are two forms of textures: simulated and actual. Simulated textures take the form of either mark-making (image 1) or photographs of textural reality (image 2). Actual texture relates more easily to three-dimensional work, as illustrated in this large garden planter. The texture flows horizontal then vertical, changing direction as it evolves around the rim (image 3).

The shallow and flat form can be put to utilitarian purposes as demonstrated in chapter 6, or used for individual expression. There is much historical reference to the open form being used for this latter reason. The following images have been selected in order that the visual vocabulary of *line*, *shape*, *colour*, *tone* and *texture* can be related to the individual selective and expressive process in their making.

Images 398, 399 and 400 are a series of large thrown shallow forms, 51 cm (20 in) in diameter. All three are landscape-orientated with different visual intentions.

Fig 398: The different shapes on the lower part of the form were created through the method of pouring glazes. The contrasting cloud shapes were brush-applied. The result is a unified tonal landscape with an intentional circular movement.

Fig 399: The intention is to have two specific focal points. This was achieved by isolating the cloud formation from the tree. The white clouds stand out vividly against the black background. The clouds are in the shape of an arch, establishing their circular relationship to the form. The tree shape has equal importance by being confined in a circle. The only link between the two is the lines, representing rain, descending from the arch-shaped clouds to the light-coloured circle.

Fig 400: This is a complex arrangement of representational and abstract shapes. The realistic clouds contrast with the geometric shapes of the circle, triangle and directional gold lines. The black linear shape conveys a strong horizontal movement with the black linear shape. This contrasts with the four delicate gold lines running vertically from top to bottom. There is also a dramatic change in scale in relation to the row of gold tree shapes at the base of the form.

All the compositional structures of images 398–400 have been explained by defining the abstract structure within a realistic arrangement. It is important to understand the underlying structure of realistic images through abstract analysis, as was demonstrated in the analyses of the photographic images at the beginning of this chapter.

Fig 401: These three images have a common identity placed within a central square configuration. Image A is an apple drawn in a realistic style using a real cut apple as a model. A black ceramic pencil was used on bisque ware, before the clear-glaze firing. Image B was sprayed with a black slip over a white clay body. The drawing was executed before firing, with a sharp metal instrument cutting through the black slip to create the white line. The intention was a very quick and impressionistic drawing, unlike in image A. The change in scale between identifiable objects was the principal motivation applied to its design. Image C was designed to give the impression of the square with the half apple being laid over the basket and bananas. The handles of the basket help to take the eye out to the edge of the form, creating a strong horizontal line through the pips of the apple, giving additional variety to the composition. This was painted with underglaze commercial colours mixed in a white base slip.

Fig 402: Image D was drawn, sitting in front of an apple tree, with a sharp instrument onto an unfired shallow form. Drawing directly from nature is exceptionally helpful in developing the selective process. The apples are drawn diagonally across the form. An intentional contrast is the placement of the leaf forms, which make an informal pattern around the diagonal placement of the apples. Image E is a large abstract pattern of coloured linear shapes working their way into the four designated corners of the form. Coloured ceramic pencils were used to draw the image onto the bisque form before the glaze firing. The intention was to have a large abstract informal pattern of lines culminating in the four corners having their own individual identity. Image F is created by pouring slips and glazes, and then fired in a process known in the ceramic world as raku. This is a very unpredictable procedure. In complete contrast to all the previous images, the quality of the piece relies on its firing and post-firing process. For this reason it appeals to many working with clay, including myself. There are many books on this subject, including Tim Andrews's book *Raku* (London: A&C Black, 2005), which I highly recommend.

Fig 403: Images G, H and I represent three forms decorated in a very direct and spontaneous manner. Even though this direct application of colour has been applied to each form, they communicate a difference in intention in their individual designs. G is a still life with textural qualities. H is a very free interpretation of a linear-drawn apple held in the centre by a black linear geometric grid. A series of vigorous circular brush strokes become an outward movement to counter the strength of the lines comprising the central apple. Image I is a surreal depiction of apples and bananas standing in a landscape environment.

Having mastered the many technical challenges inherent in the medium of clay, there will come a time when the designer must be able to develop a design vocabulary that can be applied to all visual work, both two and three-dimensional. The nine visual elements are directly linked to this design vocabulary whether the work is decorated or not. Investigating both decorated and undecorated possibilities can only add to the development of the selective process, clarify intention and lead ultimately to conclusions that satisfy personal expressive needs.

8 EXPRESSIVE APPROACHES TO BASIC THROWN FORMS:
THE CYLINDER, SPHERE AND CONE

This chapter illustrates expressive approaches that were realised over many years of investigation and experimentation with visual language applied to three basic forms. Methods of physical alteration and surface decoration resulted in a personal expression of design decisions and visual intention. The qualities achieved are the result of a harmonious unity of technical competence (throwing skills), knowledge and understanding of materials (glazes, firing processes), and drawing skills.

These are my conclusions, and as such they are not presented here to be imitated; following someone else's tenets is an unhelpful way to go about finding your own forms of expression. It is hoped that through an appreciation, and eventually an understanding, of the infinite potential contained within the basic forms presented here, you will choose to explore visual language in your own way, and you will find as much potential and creative satisfaction as I have.

404

Fig 404: These represent three basic wheel-thrown forms. Each form was thrown in a diagrammatic way, without personal expression. The sides of the cylinder and the cone are absolutely straight. Because of its curvature the sphere does not suffer from the same sterility of appearance. Design development will involve visual selection of size together with the manipulation and combination of these forms to create character and expression (see Chapter 4, illustrations 192–197).

Fig 405: Decorative or surface qualities are a way of developing expression without changing the size and/or character of the form: compare the cylinder and the cone shapes in illustration 404. The slight outward curvature of the vertical sides has enriched these forms. These minute changes have made a subtle but substantial visual difference.

The cylinder has been brush-decorated on top of poured glazes. The sphere was sprayed with underglaze colours mixed in a base slip, bits of torn paper were used as stencils, creating a pattern of coloured shapes. Then the whole object was sprayed with a clear glaze. The cone is raku-fired with poured slips and glazes. All three are dramatically different from each other without deviating greatly from their original form.

Fig 406: The ability to throw large forms is simply a matter of adding more clay to the single kilo that was used to develop throwing skills in chapter 3. This should be done in small degrees. The process of centring and lifting, along with speed control and all the basic principles related to the mechanics of the wheel, does not change. Throwing large forms, where there is very little or no support of the arms after the first lift, depends on body flexibility. The above form weighs 4 kg (8 lb 13 oz). The handle is purposely informal and fluid compared to the rather formal cylinder shape of the pitcher. The handle runs down the length of the form without necessarily being functional. Being 41 cm (16 in) in height, it is not practical as a pouring implement, and thus falls into the decorative category.

Figs 407–411: These are five examples of tall cylindrical throwing. 407 is stoneware-fired, brush-decorated and gold lustre-fired. 408 has been salt-glazed. The handle, base and inside of 409 are black-glazed. A dry white slip enables the rubber-plant drawing to be made with a black underglaze pencil. (The drawing is applied after the bisque firing.) 410 is a raku-fired cover jar with the horizontal poured glaze describing a countermovement to the vertical narrow form. Unlike the previous forms, 411 does not suggest the domestic shape of a jug or cover jar. The diagonal 'slicing' of the form's surface adds a mystery of intention and thus carries a more sculptural implication. The finished surface was smoke-fired. All the forms are 41 cm (16 in) in height. There is a clear visual variety between these forms, although the throwing procedure for each was very similar.

Manipulation of the three primary forms

Fig 412: This example illustrates how a simple thrown form can be changed through a process of flattening the form. The top rim is left to stiffen up before the hands are placed on either side and gently pushed together. The top rim can be cut and lines drawn, making additional shapes within the body of the form. Through flattening the form, the maker has the option of making a different design on each side.

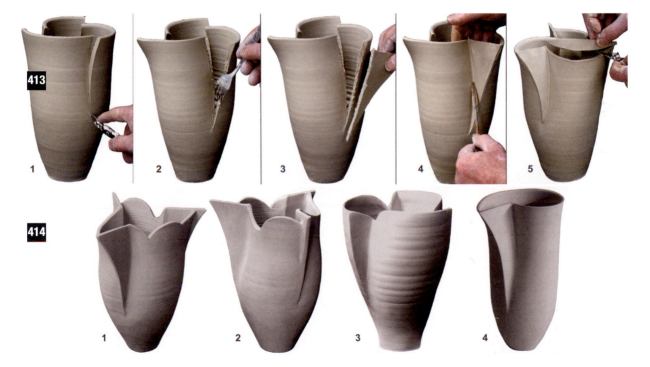

Figs 413 & 414: In image no.1 of illustration 413 the form is cut vertically into three equal sections. Leave to stiffen after throwing so that each section can be pulled out without the form collapsing. (413, image no.2) The edges where an additional piece of clay will be placed are thoroughly scratched with a fork and dampened with a sponge. The scratched area will become very soft and slushy. (413, image no.3) A flat piece of clay is cut and the edges prepared as in illustration 2. (413, image 4) All edges are pressed together both inside and out and sponged over. A metal or wooden pointed tool can be used to run down adjoining parts. The form at this stage has a symmetrical look as a result of being cut into three equal sections. It is up to the maker to decide, through visual intention, whether the form is to remain symmetrical or become asymmetrical. (413, image 5) The top is cut in an asymmetrical way as shown in the first two forms of illustration 414. In the same illustration, form 3 is symmetrical, while the simple cylinder (form 4) is asymmetrical without overmanipulation of the top rim.

Fig 415: Illustrations 1, 2, 3, 4 & 5 represent the ability to manipulate both the inside and outside of the form when the clay is at a fairly soft stage. The consistency of the clay will reflect its capacity to be pushed from either direction. De-aired clay, because of its plasticity, can be pushed further than non-de-aired clay before small cracks will appear.

Figs 416–418: The jug, cheese dish and cover jar illustrated are examples of personalising form without deviating greatly from simple basic shapes. In all three finished forms additional pieces of clay have been added. In illustration 416 a handle and pouring spout was added to the cylindrical form, denoting its function. In illustration 417 the form has a handle in the shape of a rainbow, making this cheese dish practical, with black rain clouds pushed upwards from inside the lid. In illustration 418, the form has golden cloud shapes on its lid, more a decorative motif than a functional one. The manipulations and additions have given personal expression to each work.

Fig 419: Another way of manipulating the form, working directly on the wheel, is by expressing informality. When trying this technique, it may help to throw in a formal way to begin with, as in the first illustration. With the wheel revolving very slowly, push from the inside and outside to make off-centre figurations. With a bit of practice, this can become a fun thing to do. A helpful approach would be to throw about 20 of these loose forms, line them up together, and exercise your selective process using critical assessment. This will allow you to make better design decisions and clarify a way forward with regard to your intention. The shallow form is also good for this way of working.

Each form, whether cylinder, sphere, cone or open form, can be manipulated or combined together for expressive reasons. The maker decides whether the way to communicate their intention is best expressed through the purity of the basic form or otherwise.

Fig 420: This small spherical form is being manipulated from the outside using the fingers as the drawing tool. Trial and error is the only way to know when the condition of the clay is ready for this type of figuration. The quality of line – whether it is pressed deeply or lightly into the form – is a matter of the maker's selective process. These lines were designed to be sympathetic to the spherical shape by flowing around the form rather than being ridged.

Fig 421: The cylindrical form flattened in illustration 412 was done so easily with the hands because of the open top. The spherical form, because of its small neck, is better flattened with two boards. The boards are gently worked back and forth until the desired shape is made. The neck is left to harden to a degree before any attempt is made to flatten the form. This will prevent the form from collapsing. The flattening process is done very slowly because, if done quickly, the air trying to escape from the inside is likely to cause the form to split. After the flattened form hardens the circle and line can be carved into the surface.

Working within a theme

Fig 422: The off-centring of the circular figuration has brought the two circles closer together. Symmetry still exists when the two forms are placed side by side. Within the circles the asymmetrical pattern of clouds and rays of sunlight is deliberately different in each form. The intention is to play symmetry against asymmetry using nature as the central theme. A common theme can unify a body of work, though the forms may not be identical to each other (images 422–429 will illustrate this point).

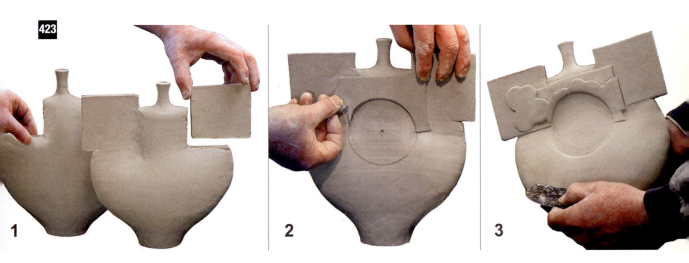

Fig 423: In image no.1, the corners of the flattened form have been cut out and pinched together, allowing squares of flat clay to be placed in the vacant positions. (image no.2) Another flat piece of clay is placed on top of the circle. Follow the same procedure of assembly as in illustration 413. The flat piece of clay and the flattened form must be at the same consistency, firm but not too dry. Cracking will occur in the drying stages if one piece is much dryer than the other. The assembled form can also be wrapped in polythene overnight, which will help to equalise all the pieces. (image no.3) When the assembled form is just about dry, it is time to finish the surface. A metal rib can be used, followed by a thorough sponging. If the clay is bone dry, there will be considerable dust as you scrape the surface. This is very unhealthy to breathe. If it is necessary to work clay in a dry state, wear a respirator. Clay, with stabilising materials like grog, sand or molochite, which are larger than 120-mesh size, acquires a rough surface when scraped and sponged. If the particles are larger than 120 mesh, after scraping the rib can also be used to press these materials back into the surface of the body as long as the clay is not bone dry.

Fig 424: These are three examples of assembled flattened forms continuing the theme of nature. All three forms are symmetrically orientated. The first two forms are asymmetrically carved, while the third is symmetrical but tends to lose the identity of the spherical form due to the extent of clay applied on either side. This is an example of theme development with the intention of building onto the flattened bottle form.

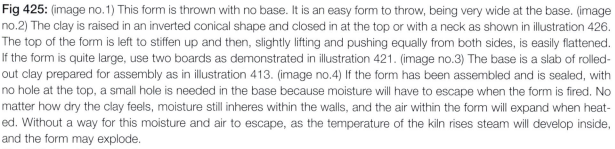

Fig 425: (image no.1) This form is thrown with no base. It is an easy form to throw, being very wide at the base. (image no.2) The clay is raised in an inverted conical shape and closed in at the top or with a neck as shown in illustration 426. The top of the form is left to stiffen up and then, slightly lifting and pushing equally from both sides, is easily flattened. If the form is quite large, use two boards as demonstrated in illustration 421. (image no.3) The base is a slab of rolled-out clay prepared for assembly as in illustration 413. (image no.4) If the form has been assembled and is sealed, with no hole at the top, a small hole is needed in the base because moisture will have to escape when the form is fired. No matter how dry the clay feels, moisture still inheres within the walls, and the air within the form will expand when heated. Without a way for this moisture and air to escape, as the temperature of the kiln rises steam will develop inside, and the form may explode.

Fig 426: Continuing the theme of nature, the decoration on these images depends on the quality of drawing. The skill required to throw a well-constructed form is comparable to developing the skills needed to translate ideas through drawing. Indeed, the two skills complement each other and logically should be developed together. Drawing has been referred to in illustration 420 where fingers are used as the drawing tool. Any marks applied to the form could be considered as drawing. The carved half-circles on both forms and the carved cloud formation on the rear form can all be classified as an application of drawing. In fact the unity and balance between form and mark-making or drawing is what will decide the ultimate success of the piece.

Group no.1

Group no.2

Fig: 427 Group no.1 is a three-piece composition. The decoration is meant to flow from one form to the other. A flattened form, like the one in the centre, was cut in half and the top discarded, creating the smaller front form. The scale and positioning of the three forms was carefully considered before decoration was applied. Off-centring the position of the forms enabled the rain drawing to be easily seen on the largest form, and also creates a strong vertical pattern. This vertical is echoed in the fine gold lines running from the middle form to the smallest. Positioning, colour and decorative motif have produced a unified group of related forms.

Group no.2 is a composition of three forms that are more individual in relation to each other than image no.1. The middle form was cut out from a thrown form similar to the largest one, and reassembled with flat pieces of clay using the same techniques as in illustration 423. The textural horizontal movement in the central form gives a conclusion to the vertical movement of the silver tree shape. The informality of these silver lines acts as a visual counterpoint to the formality of all three forms within this composition.

Fig: 427A A composition of three units expressing a horizontal rhythm passing through the centre of two supporting flattened bottle forms. An additional movement of small vertical lines can be seen in the centre where the flattened forms meet. This leads on to the smaller central form, which becomes an exaggerated golden waterfall. The waterfall, in terms of both vertical movement and scale, brings the vision downwards, thus unifying the three forms.

Fig 428: (image no.1) This slightly conical form is 36 cm (14 in) high. (image no.2) A torch fuelled from a propane tank (or a hand-held blow torch) can be used to stiffen the clay so that the entire form can be completed immediately (thus obviating the need to wait at least a day until the form is strong enough to support the addition of a top piece). The wheel is kept revolving slowly while being heated. It is highly recommended that you position the propane tank outside the room you are working in, at the end of a long hose connection. The image is included simply to show where the flame is coming from. (image no.3) Another piece is thrown without a base and measured by calipers. (image no.4) The top of the tall form is measured to make sure it conforms to image no.3.

Fig 428A: (image no.5) The top is prepared for assembly. (image no.6) The conical shape, when thrown, was not cut from the bat that was on top of the wheel. Being firmly stuck to the bat, it can be turned over without falling off. (image no.7) The bat can now be cut off. (image no.8) The two forms are secured to each other by pressing from the inside and running the rib up and down at the joint.

Fig 428B: (image no.9) A shallow form is then thrown. (image nos 10 & 11). With both hands fold over the shallow form. (image no.12) The ends can be raised in this manner if desired. This folded form was used for numerous pieces of various scales (see garden sculpture, illustration 439).

Fig 429: These two works have been derived from the basic composite form shown in illustration 428. The series of finished works within chapters 7 and 8 have struck a balance between the techniques of throwing and the application of design, in relation both to individual work and the development of a variety of forms adapted to extend the expression of a chosen theme.

Fig 430: This large open form follows the same procedure as the composite form in illustration 428.

Fig 431: The base is trimmed and a small cylindrical form is thrown for the foot. The same procedure would also be used for adding another section to a form, irrespective of the size.

Fig 432: This large open form is 50 cm (20 in) in diameter and 35 cm (14 in) in height. The same technique of cutting and assembling was used as in illustration 413.

Fig 433: (Image no.1) A thin board is pressed on both sides of a small, thick piece of clay, making a border. (Image no.2) A flat-headed screwdriver was used to make these marks in the clay. A sharp instrument like a knife tends not to separate the marks as well as something blunter. (Image no.3) The clay pattern is pulled out with a throwing motion. The clay hits the canvas surface and is pulled at the same time at a very low angle. (Image no.4) In the process of being thrown out, the clay will become thinner. Practice will determine how thin the clay can become before breaking. De-aired clay will extend much further than non-de-aired clay because of its plasticity.

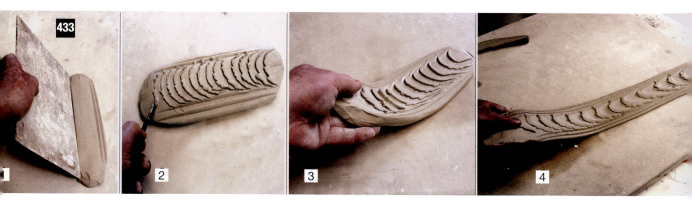

Fig 434: (Image no.1) The pattern of clay is then lifted and attached to the large form. (Image no.2) The clay pattern can be attached from outside or inside the form. (Image no.3) Patterns and textures can be developed through experimenting with different tools and objects pressed into the clay before it is stretched out. The clay when stretched in this manner has less of a mechanical look, perhaps as though it has been weathered by nature.

Fig 435: Three very large garden planters, each one 65 cm (26 in) in diameter, with the tallest being 80 cm (32 in) in height. The bases were separately thrown, with a decorative strip applied to the top edges, giving the appearance of a single unit rather than one form sitting on top of the other. Thus the upper forms were thrown without needing to be trimmed at the bottom. The bases are simple cylinders that also needed no trimming. The possibilities for patterns and textural motifs are infinite. When such a wide choice is available, the selective process becomes of paramount importance.

Fig 436: (Image no.1) These two forms are larger but no different in manufacture than those in illustration 425. The bases have been left off to allow the forms to be manipulated from the inside. Image no.2 is an oversize fruit basket, with the drawing of the apples and bananas from the inside. A strip of clay simulating a wicker basket was applied underneath the fruit. This was made by throwing out a piece of clay as demonstrated in illustration 433. Image no.3 shows a platform with a hole cut into the supporting board, enabling the arm to reach up into the hollow clay form. This platform was also used when making the fruit basket. The bases are fitted in the same manner as illustrated in 425.

Fig 437: This is part of a group of 15 figurative forms. The finished surface is a dark-grey slip which unified the group. Lighting was a critical factor in creating an atmosphere when these were displayed. The small neck conclusion has been used on many forms, with nature as the theme (see illustrations 422–427A). A particular shape or conclusion, like the small neck, can become compelling, for no logical reason to be returned to time and again. Consciously or unconsciously, a detail like the neck can become a hallmark of one's work. From the simple flattened form as shown in illustration 436, image no.1, a multitude of different expressive movements have been modelled to define individuality in each figure.

Fig 438–439: Developing your identity through your work is very much an outcome of individual expression and is greatly to be encouraged. This book has promoted the necessity of integrating discipline, perseverance, technique and design as a foundation to eventually achieving this end. Discipline can be measured through practice over time. Perseverance is measured through increasing technical proficiency.

Finding individual solutions to design problems will always provide the greatest challenges in forging an identity in your work. Inherent in this are the visual decisions you make (your intention and selection) and your ability to remain open and critical in assessing your work.

This evaluation and assessment is what I call my *design vocabulary*, which I apply to the construction of all two-dimensional or three-dimensional works, regardless of medium or scale. It is immaterial whether I am doing domestic ceramics, as in illustration 438, or garden sculpture, as in illustration 439. The vocabulary for solving issues of design is identical in every visual medium.

INSPIRATION FROM SOURCE MATERIAL

It is essential that the craft worker develops their unique and recognizable style. This takes time and should not be a priority until fundamental techniques are mastered in conjunction with constant application of visual language. This book concentrates specifically on techniques associated with the potter's wheel, and the introduction to visual language (chapters 7-8) for compositional organisation. The quest for your own development and style needs a starting point. Source material in most cases provides this and can be defined by asking a simple question: what am I interested in? This forces the maker to reflect deeply on their creative practice, leading to a process of research not unlike other forms of rigorous research carried out in other disciplines. The 'truths' that are eventually revealed and applied visually are critical to the work produced and ultimately give the work its recognised quality and integrity.

Forms of source material may take the form of writing, photographs, sketches, drawings, trials, samples and experimentation, all documented for the sole purpose of revealing ideas that can be realised visually either two- or three-dimensionally in the finished work. Work that visually communicates your intentions, provides inspiration, stimulates further investigation and engages the viewer. The end result (your findings) will, over time, constitute a body of work through which both the maker and the viewer can recognise identity or style through a sense of visual attraction.

The work's origins or source is embedded in the maker's personal interests and forms the basis for future research. Source material is the cornerstone of creative evolution, a non-linear cyclical involvement that includes interests/inspiration, ideas, research, experimentation, statement, identity. This cycle will never begin without excellent technique, visual language and human qualities such as discipline, dedication and desire.

FIVE POTTERS: Inspirations And Working Methods

440

441

The five potters represented have a strong commitment to creating their work using the wheel, but do not exclude other techniques for creating ceramic forms. They have been identified for their dedication to fine craftsmanship, and the individuality expressed in their work. Tony Laverick (porcelain), Tim Andrews (raku), Susan Hall (earthenware), Fergus Stewart (salt glaze) and David Grant (stoneware) have given an insight into their inspirations, working methods and creative processes. These statements communicate a process of investigation, refinement, and a search for new horizons to keep the work alive and growing both for themselves and the viewer.

Fig: 440 *Upright Porcelain Bowl*, ht: 40.5 cm (16 in). The translucency can be seen well on this form.
Fig: 441 *Porcelain Vessel*, ht: 46 cm (18 in). This was pushed and distorted just after being thrown. This does make turning at leatherhard stage difficult but not impossible. Opaque glaze.

TONY LAVERICK

I was born near Sunderland in 1961. I studied Ceramics at Preston Polytechnic. Although it was mainly a studio ceramics course, it involved a good grounding in all aspects of ceramics, including Industrial Ceramics. I was grateful for this when, on leaving college, I was offered a job in a small factory in Stoke-on-Trent as a designer, where I stayed for two years. This was followed by two years at Coalport China (part of the Wedgwood Group). This proved to be invaluable experience when I left to set up on my own in 1988.

All of my work is thrown and turned porcelain (occasionally slabbed), onto which I apply precious-metal lustres in multiple refirings.

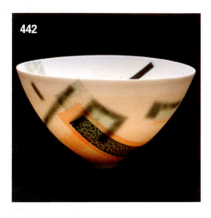

442

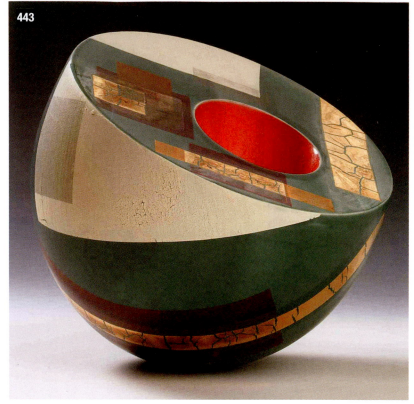

443

444

Fig: 442 Porcelain Bowl, ht: 25 cm (10 in), dia: 30 cm (12 in). Similar in shape to 440 but smaller. When lit from behind the translucency is more apparent.

Fig: 443 Porcelain form, ht: 25 cm (10 in). Opaque glaze.

Fig: 444 Porcelain form, ht: 38 cm (15 in). Thrown and turned.

More recently, I have been firing bisque to 1270°C (2318°F) with glaze and lustre firings progressively lower. I am influenced by contemporary potters but, because of my background as a designer in the ceramics industry, I have a broader appreciation of ceramics, notably fine examples of art ceramics produced at the end of the 19th century and 20th century by Royal Doulton, Ruskin, Bernard Moore, Moorcroft and Pilkington's Royal Lancastrian lustreware. Also many French potters such as August Delaherche and Clement Massier. I find I am influenced by 20th century art as much as ceramics, artists like Kandinsky, Malevich, Mondrian, Nicholson and Brancusi and this is reflected in my work.

As each piece of my work is unique, you can detect the constant change. I am constantly seeking to expand my own limits, pushing boundaries and taking the risks that are necessary for growth. I have not become seduced into a production-workshop mentality where exact repetition of the known is the dominant factor. It is the willingness to take risks and bear the consequences that distinguishes the artist from the craftsman.

Fig: 445 Porcelain form, ht: 20 cm (8 in). Opaque glaze. These forms are thrown in two parts. The top or flat section (with red hollow) is thrown upside down with the bottom part thrown as a bowl. Then the two parts are joined.

What inspires the maker through their source material must be analysed and understood through compositional organisation to avoid superficial duplication of the source itself. I will use Tony Laverick's work to explore this and describe compositional organisation from a visual perspective.

Tony Laverick's statement includes a comprehensive list of source material from both industry and individuals working with ceramics, and a list of painters and sculptors associated with the world of fine art. Influences and source material are not necessarily evident to the viewer unless accompanied by the maker's statement, and even then the viewer may not be familiar with names. What are evident to the viewer are the qualities within the piece. These qualities, whether defined through knowledge or association, are the foundation for the viewer's reaction to the work. The individual pieces (illustrations 440–45) are visually evaluated through the quality of his forms: their elegance, the sense of floating due to their narrow bases and the thinness of the porcelain, which allows light to pass through the pieces, expressing the nature of the material. The red circular indentations in illustrations 443 and 445 give an impression of hollowness, which also denote a strong visual focal point. All are abstract, using geometric composition in the design, with various degrees of colours and shapes applied to the porcelain bodies. Illustrations 440, 441 and 442 are open forms which have the additional dimension of revealing both the inside and outside at the same time. These pieces all encourage the viewer to rotate them, even slightly, so as to be confronted with different visual relationships of shape.

I have experienced Tony Laverick's work in relation to my *visual reading* of the forms, by recognising the visual elements within the compositional structure (and applying my visual language). Whether or not the work is stimulated by source material as an initial starting point, it is the compositional organisation of the pieces which will determine its ultimate success.

Compositional organization as relates to the remaining four potters is for the reader of this book to analyse for themselves. It is important that everything which is visual can be visually read by analysing its physical structure (what can be seen). Over time and gathered experience, visual vocabulary, when applied to what is seen, becomes increasingly acute.

Fig: 446 Pot being extracted from the kiln (normally this should be done using tongs). Raku-fired.

TIM ANDREWS

Throwing has always been at the heart of my potting life. As a keen teenager, my first purchase was an old momentum wheel, bought for five pounds. It had a flywheel made from a cartwheel and a carved wooden tractor seat that I almost needed a stepladder to mount. The throwing head was cast from plaster of Paris and I had to be careful to avoid scraping bits of it into the rusty, polythene-lined tray.

My professional career began in the 1970s with an apprenticeship with David Leach. He was an expert at teaching production throwing. I learnt about economy of movement, distribution of the clay, the rhythm of working, subtlety of form and line, balance, lift and so on. I made many thousands of pieces from David's extensive range of domestic stoneware, gradually progressing to more complex forms and eventually making his most demanding porcelain bowls, cups and saucers, and teapots, all on a kick-wheel. It was a rigorous training, one from which a willing student was able to learn fast. It is arguable whether it is possible to gain the same confidence as quickly through other means. It was about learning a three-dimensional visual language, one that has stood me in good stead since. These days I often break these 'rules', but when I do it is usually a conscious and informed decision stemming from a sound basis of knowledge. Of course sometimes it's also worth having a blind stab in the dark at something just to shake things up a bit. As David Leach used to say, 'let the pendulum swing wildly occasionally'.

I went on to Dartington for a further two years' training. It was a chance to widen my aesthetic range as well as broaden my skill base. Eventually I set up my first studio and for some years designed and produced a range of my own functional porcelain and stoneware. Nearly three decades later, having moved away from making purely utilitarian ware, my pieces have become more individual and consequently much more labour-intensive. As a proportion of the time spent on each piece, the throwing is now only a small part. Burnishing, slip work, glazing and raku firings take increasingly longer as the pieces have become more complex. However, throwing is still an integral part of my making process, now often combined with handbuilding and other methods. These days I regard the wheel as being a familiar tool, literally a 'kicking off' point from which to begin exploring design ideas, not to dictate them.

Fig: 447 *Black and White Striped Humbug*, dia: approx. 25 cm (10 in). Raku-fired with resist decoration.
Fig: 448 Tim Andrews applying tape for resist technique.

Along with the move away from function I chose to use the raku process as my main firing technique. This in itself has altered my approach to throwing. In general now, I increase the wall thickness for pieces that are to be raku fired. There are two reasons for this. The first is that a thin wall tends to absorb smoke too readily. This can be a problem when I am trying to keep areas of the surface unsmoked by using a resist slip and glaze. If smoke penetration is too great these areas tend to become grey and 'dirty' looking and I lose the good contrast between black and white. A thicker wall helps to prevent this from happening as the smoke does not penetrate right through the body. The second reason is to do with the weight of a piece. When potters first learn to throw they are nearly always encouraged to make the pot as light as possible. It's generally good advice. After all, a stoneware or porcelain teapot shouldn't feel full of tea when it's empty. Such ware becomes dense and consequently heavy after firing, and the glaze alone can make up nearly half the weight of a high-fired piece. For me there is an appropriate weight for any pot – one that 'feels right' – so a less dense, possibly unglazed raku piece may need to be potted a little thicker to acheive its optimum weight.

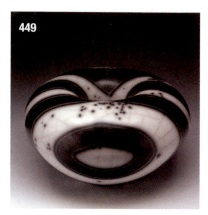

Some forms may begin on the wheel but are then cut or distorted, shaped by hand or joined. Throwing a very thick-walled pot allows me to cut slices from it using a taught wire while it is wet. Similarly, I may throw a 'beehive' or spherical shape that is subsequently cut and shaped into a sculptural form. In these pieces all evidence of throwing may ultimately be lost. Burnishing a piece also affects its finished 'mood'. If it is done on the wheel the marks made accentuate the throwing process, but there is a possibility of an over-machined looking surface. Hand burnishing produces a subtle, slightly distorted surface that bears marks that give a piece a richer, more human feeling.

Fig: 449 *Large Wide-striped Humbug*, dia: approx. 40 cm (15¾ in).
Fig: 450 *Lidded Curling Pieces*, ht: 55 cm (22 in) and 48 cm (19 in).

Fig: 451 *Pale Blue and Black Striped Humbug*, dia: 32 cm (12½ in).
Fig: 452 *Angled Lidded Curling Pieces*, dia: (largest) 25 cm (10 in).

JENNIFER HALL

The ongoing aim is to develop a comprehensive range of pots that would enliven the daily rituals of taking nourishment. These pots were not to challenge but to comfort and enrich food times for people who live to eat, not eat to live. It is the immediacy of producing pots on a wheel that appeals to me. The restrictions of throwing, and the techniques and skills involved, provide me with the boundaries in production and development which I like to work to.

I am drawn to earthenware with its warmth of colour and softness of edge. It also appeals to me because of its suitability to electric firing at convenient low temperatures. Early on I established that my interests lay in the making and decorating rather than in the firing process itself. After the efforts and time applied when the clay is at the leatherhard and bisque stages, I need a reliable firing method.

My inspiration comes from a collection of images from natural and manmade environments (various leaf shapes or traditional milk churns for instance). These I collect as photographs, sketches or stored in my subconscious. The overwhelming influence upon the form is its

Fig: 453 3 lb jug, ht: 16 cm (6¼ in). Earthenware, with slip-trailed leaf and cobalt detail.

Fig: 454 Large (2½ pint) and small (1½ pint) teapots, ht: 19 cm (7½ in) and 13.5 cm (5¼ in). Slip decorated with abstract design.

Fig: 455 Honey pot, mustard pot and butter dish. Earthenware with sgraffito decoration.

Fig: **456** Bread crock, ht: 35 cm (14 in). Slip-decorated earthenware with abstract design.

Fig: **457** Casserole dish with sgraffito scabious leaf design, ht: 17 cm (6¾ in).

Fig: **458** Flower troughs, with slip trail and sgraffito decoration, ht: 18 cm (7 in).

function. Inspiration is provided by vessels of glass, metal and clay, both ancient and modern, and designed for similar use. (These I have found in various locations, particularly museums and galleries.) Further to this the pots are informed by my own throwing abilities, the nature of the materials and the stages of the making processes. My dislike of 'turning', for instance, has forced me to develop a range of shapes without turned foot-rings, so ribs are used to create beading at the base of many of my pots. This not only provides a good finish, but also provides a place for fingers when dipping in slip and glaze.

Not to decorate earthenware seems like a wasted opportunity. The materials readily lend themselves to layering a range of decorative techniques, building up a lively surface before applying glaze.

Initially, all decoration related to leaf motifs and smothered the forms. My decoration is now becoming more sparse and relates more to the form, perhaps as my throwing abilities develop and my forms gain confidence.

At leatherhard, a layering of slip decoration is applied by pouring, dipping, brushing, trailing and sgraffito. Sometimes five techniques are used on the same pot. This initial decoration provides a depth, which in combination with the non-toxic lead glazes (fired at 1060°C/1940°F and soaked) in turn provides colour and fluidity. Although each pot has several layers of decoration, some applied before the bisque stage, some after, each stage is relatively speedy. Nothing is laboured over, as I believe the decoration is at its best when executed rapidly and with confidence. Although the firing process is predictable to a point, the results may vary as the thickness of the slips are judged by feel, and the thinner the slip, the more the red clay blushes through.

FERGUS STEWART

I am very mindful of history and ceramic tradition, and seek to interpret and contribute rather than mimic. I was introduced to pottery and ceramics at high school, and was inspired by the contents of a local ceramics collector's kitchen. Pots of Anglo-Oriental tradition, mixed with large jugs, jars and salt-glazed crocks from French and English country potteries, and a selection of teapots and handmade utensils of all sorts fought for space with early bowls from Korea and China in the clutter of their daily use and storage. These influences remain within my work today.

Over time, I have developed a diverse repertoire of domestic and decorative forms that employ a comprehensive range of traditional pottery skills in their making and firing, creating a family of forms related through shared characteristics within the design, making and firing, sometimes challenging traditional concepts about use and the presentation of food.

My work has developed through repetition and refinement in the pursuit of designing and making useful handmade objects which, when well considered and sensitively made, communicate very directly and intimately with their user, offering a link to our pre-industrial past, whilst conveying notions about intention and attitude, and affirming values of human patience and skill. I work primarily at the wheel, throwing, altering and constructing by joining thrown forms to slabs and stretched, thrown components. Many forms are finished away from the wheel by cutting and carving.

Fig: 459 *Tea Jars*, ht: 16 cm (6¼ in). Black and orange slips, wood-fired saltglaze, fired to 1320°C (2408°F).
Fig: 460 *Tea For One*, ht: 14 cm (5½ in). Black slip, wood-fired saltglaze, fired to 1320°C (2408°F).

Fig: 461 Faceted bowl in progress.
Fig: 462 Basket Form Vase, ht: 32 cm (12½ in). Black/blue slip, wood-fired saltglaze, fired to 1320°C (2408°F).
Fig: 463 For Schnapps, ht: 16 cm (6¼ in). Porcelain and stoneware with redclay slips, wood-fired saltglaze, fired to 1320°C (2408°F).

Decorating and creating surfaces often incorporates local materials, with coloured slips and glaze in the green and bisque stages.

I am drawn to the qualities of wood-fired ceramics and have explored the variety within glazed, anagama and salt-glazed surfaces and firing procedures, designing and building kilns for

Fig: 464 Oval container, ht: 10 cm (4 in). Orange slip, wood-fired and salt-glazed to 1320°C (2408°F).

Fig: 465 Citrus juicer and vinaigrette bowl. Red clay slips and shino glaze interior.

Fig: 466 Oval containers, ht: 12 cm (4¾ in). Wood-fired and salt-glazed to 1320°C (2408°F).

specific results, and making and exhibiting significant bodies of work in each specialisation.

In 1997, it was time to reassess the nature and direction of my studio practice and its location in Australia. I began travelling back to Scotland regularly to work and teach, and in 2002 made plans to resettle in the Scottish Highlands, where I feel a strong connection and spirit of place which, I feel, will also continue to influence the creative development of my work. I am currently developing a range of coloured and variously textured slips for salt glaze, using porcelain and stoneware clay bodies for a new generation of work, and have built a smaller-scale two-chamber wood-burning kiln to fire work for exhibition and continued research and development.

Born in Aberdeen, Scotland, I began working with clay while at high school in Dumfries & Galloway. Following studio-based training as a domestic-wares potter I emigrated to Australia, firstly working at Beaufort Pottery, Perth, Western Australia, then establishing a studio and building my first wood-fired kiln during 1984 in the same city. I later relocated to Canberra, where I co-founded the Strathnairn Ceramics access workshop, and continued my studio practice there until 2001. I returned to Scotland in 2002, re-establishing my studio practice in the scenic location of Assynt in the North-west Highlands.

Fig: 467 Thrown lidded jar by Ruth Goldie, ht: 30.5 cm (12 in). Red glaze decorated with rowan berries.
Fig: 468 (Left) Bowl by Tracey Montgomery. Decorated with anemones.
(Centre and right) Plate and bowl by Dorell Pirie, dia: 25.5 cm (10 in). Decorated with petunias.

DAVID GRANT

I was born in the North-west Highlands of Scotland, and studied ceramics in Dundee and London until 1974, when Highland Stoneware (Scotland) Ltd was formed, with Royal College of Art tutors, Grahame Clarke and the Marquess of Queensberry as fellow directors. At the moment we employ 25 for a workforce doing a cross section of different ceramic operations. Highland Stoneware is, we hope, an organized structure within which there is great freedom to innovate and experiment. This is mainly, but not exclusively, in freehand painted decoration. Hand throwing is of course the making method most entirely reliant on the skill and technique of the potter. Along with throwing, we also use jigger and jolley, and extrusions which form the trilogy of our working processes.

The evolution in what we make, from undecorated tableware in the mid-70s to the multiplicity of decoration themes we make today, has a number of motivating forces. Many of the themes are inspired by, and grow from, our environment. Successful decoration themes such as Seascape, Landscape, Fish, Rock Pools, Poppy, Puffin, Iris, Wild Berry, Sheep, Pebbles, Thistle, and a large number of floral decorations based on local flowers may illustrate the point. A multiplicity of talents have been applied, but despite diverse starting points, comments are frequently made that there is a homogeny to it all, a 'Highland Stoneware' look, but also that our work is very much 'of the area', in a sense the beginning of a tradition (and they all begin at some time).

'Seascape' and 'Landscape' account for nearly one third of our

Fig: 469 Thrown jug by Fergus Stewart, ht: 33 cm (13 in). Decorated with cat by Dorrell Pirie.

Fig: 470 Bread crock by David Grant. Seascape design.

Fig: 471 Wall plate by Tricia Thom. Design in 17th century Delft tradition.

Fig: 472 Jigger and jolley charger, dia: 30.5 cm (12 in). 'White Water' decoration theme.

Fig: 473 Thrown vase, ht: 41 cm (16 in). White narcissus painted by Lesley Thorpe.

Fig: 474 Jugs thrown by Fergus Stewart. Feisty 'Cockerel' design painted by Linda MacLeod.

Fig: 475 Vase by Tricia Thom, dia: 27 cm (10½ in). Early development of 'Vase of Flowers' theme by Tricia Thom.

annual production, and within these headings the variety is infinite. Landscape is virtually reinvented as decorators develop their individual approach, as any artist would if the medium was painting on canvas. Going for a walk can bring a new idea to add to the vocabulary, and certainly being on our beaches gives that overall feeling of space and perspective.

Having to make every stroke and movement count, I think, helps the final quality of the piece. Being under a bit of pressure to get through a workload is fairly normal and must not lead to hashing or rushing, but thinking through and sequencing efficient output can be a pleasure. Loading a big brush to do all of the white on a piece using different strokes as the colour dries, or putting a small sponge mark of a colour on many pieces at a time, makes for a different type of work, all many miles from designing on a drawing board.

Someone once said, 'The essence of creative activity is 1% inspiration and 99% perspiration.' There is nothing associated with the fundamentals of throwing or the application of design to the ceramic form that will be easy to achieve or quickly understood. The integral application of design in the process of making is refinement over time through critical assessment. Inspiration remains abstract and can only be assessed through the process of making.

In order to succeed as a wheel-based potter, it is hoped that a few basic truths are realised: that the process of throwing cannot exist without clay; that technique and design are inseparable; that inspiration and source material can be better developed through an understanding of compositional organisation and that determination, along with constant evaluation, will eventually expose the quest for individual expression over time. If you can understand these values (and this book should help you do that) and practise with consistency, you will achieve great satisfaction and a lifetime of creative discovery.

SUPPLIERS LIST

UK Ceramic Suppliers

Bath Potter's Supplies
Unit 18, Forth Avenue,
Westfield Trading Estate,
Radstock, BA3 4XE
Tel: 01761 411077
www.bathpotters.demon.co.uk

Briar Wheels and Suppliers Ltd
Whitsbury Road, Fordingbridge,
Hants, SP 1NQ
Tel: 01425 652991
www.briarwheels.co.uk

Brick House Ceramic Supplies
The Barn, Sheepcotes Lane,
Silver End, Witham,
Essex, CM8 3PJ
Tel: 01376 585655
www.brickhouseceramics.co.uk

Ceramtech Ltd
Units 16 & 17 Frontier Works,
33 Queen Street, Tottenham North,
London, N17 8JA
Tel: 0208 885 4492
www.ceramatech.co.uk

Commercial Clay Ltd
Sandbach Road, Cobridge, Stoke-
on-Trent, Staffs ST6 2DR
Tel: 01782 274448
www.commercialclay.co.uk

Cromartie Kilns Ltd
Park Hall Industrial Estate,
Park Hall Road, Longton
Stoke-on-Trent, Staffs ST3 5AY
Tel: 0208 885 4492
www.cromartie.co.uk

Potclays Ltd
Brick Kiln Lane, Etruria,
Stoke-on-Trent, Staffs, ST4 7B
Tel 01782 219816
www.potclays.co.uk

Potterycrafts Ltd
Campbell Road, Stoke-on-Trent,
Staffs, ST4 4ET
Tel: 01782 745000
www.potterycrafts.co.uk

Scarva Pottery Supplies
Unit 20, Scarva Road Industrial
Estate, Banbridge, Co. Down
BT32 3QD
Tel: 01820 669699
www.scarvapottery.com

Valentines Clay Products
The Sliphouse
Birches Head Road, Hanley,
Stoke-on-Trent, Staffs ST1 6LH
Tel: 01782 271200
www.valentineclays.co.uk

W J Doble Pottery Clays
Newdowns Sand and Clay Pits
St.Agnes, Cornwall TR5 0ST
Tel: 01872 552979

North American Suppliers

American Art Clay Company
4717 W.16th Street,
Indianapolis, IN 46222,
Tel: (800) 374-1600/(317) 244-6871
www.amaco.com

A.R.T Studio Clay Company
9320 Michigan Avenue,
Sturterant, WI 53177-2425,
Tel: (262) 884-4278
www.artclay.com

Axner Pottery Supply
PO Box 621484,
Oviedo, FL 32762-1484,
Tel: (800) 843-7057/(407) 365-2600
www.axner.com

Duncan Ceramics Products Inc.
5673 E. Shields Ave., Fresno,
California, 93727
Tel: (800) 237-2642/(559) 291 4444

Laguna Clay Company
14400 Lomitas Avenue,
City of Industry, CA 91746
Tel: (800) 452-4862
www.lagunaclay.com

Mile Hi Ceramics
77 Lipan, Denver, Colorado,
80223-1580
Tel: (303) 825-4570
www.milehiceramics.com

The Potter's Shop
31 Thorpe Road, Needham,
Massachusettes, MA 02194
Tel: (017) 449-7687
www.thepottersshop.com

Tucker's Pottery Supplies Inc.,
Unit 7, 15 West Pearce Street,
Richmond Hill,
Ontario, Canada L4B 1H6
Tel: 1 905 889-7705
www.tuckerspottery.com

INDEX

Anderson, Scott 6
Andrews, Tim 129, 132, 133, 134
asymmetrical 115,119,120
anticlockwise 37

base trimmer 44, 45, 51
bat 63, 64, 66
bentonite 10
bisque firing 83
blow torch 123
body 54, 65, 72, 86, 88, 89, 95, 97, 115
bowl form 66, 67, 71, 83

callipers 84, 85, 90, 91, 123
casserole 98
centrifugal force 25, 39, 42, 57
centring 32, 34, 71, 113
China clay 10
chuck 89
clay 10, 11, 15, 16, 100, 116, 142
    particles 13, 15
    commercial 12, 17
    composition 131, 142
    refined 11, 13, 14, 16, 17
colour 100, 101, 102, 103, 106, 107, 111
concave 52, 53
conical shape 29, 31, 32, 38, 42, 60, 61,
    87, 93, 112, 113, 117
convex 52, 53, 93
cover jar 95, 97, 98
critical assessment 48–51, 58, 61, 99,
    117, 127, 142
cutting wire 22, 44, 45, 46, 66
cylinder 28, 31, 35, 37, 39, 41, 43, 44, 46,
    47, 48, 49, 50, 54, 59, 60, 61, 62, 65,
    93, 98, 112, 113, 115,117, 125

de-aired clay 116, 124
de-airing pug 12, 18, 21, 79
design 48, 54, 75, 83, 102, 103, 109, 111,
    112, 115, 117, 123, 127, 131, 142
dough mixer 12
doughnut shape 36
drawing 102,109,114,120

earthenware 129, 135, 136
electric wheel 24, 27
extruding machine 78, 79
    handles 78, 79, 83

feldspathic rock 10
filter press 12, 18

firing temperature 17
flange 90, 91, 92, 95
flat open form 70, 98, 107
fly wheel 24, 25, 26, 27, 31
foot 72
form 23, 38, 54, 56, 68, 75, 99, 100, 102,
    108, 110, 112, 113, 115, 117, 120,
    125, 126, 128, 131
found clay 11, 13, 14, 17
functional ware 72, 83, 99, 116

geometric shape 108
Grant, David 129, 140, 141, 142

Hall, Jennifer 129, 135, 136
Hamer, Frank and Janet 10
handles 77–83, 87, 91, 97, 99,113
hole maker 96

imaginary centre 31, 32, 33, 34, 43
intention 28, 48, 49, 50, 57, 58, 61, 72,
    99, 108, 109, 110, 111, 112, 114,
    115, 117, 119, 120, 127, 128
iron oxide 10

jug (pitcher) 76, 83, 87, 91, 97, 98, 114

kick-wheel 24, 25, 26, 27, 132
kiln 17
knob 86, 87, 92, 98, 99

Laverick, Tony 129, 130, 131
Leach, David 132
Leach-style wheel 26
lids 84, 86, 87, 89, 90, 91, 92, 93, 95, 98,
    99, 116
lifting process 37, 40, 41, 42

mug 75, 83, 87, 91, 98

open form 36, 62, 64, 65, 66 68, 69, 72,
    71, 73, 93, 98, 104, 107, 108, 110,
    117, 123

particle size 10
Picasso 102
plaster disc 63, 64
plaster slab 15, 16, 18, 19, 20, 23
plasticity 10, 16, 78
plywood disc 64, 66
porcelain 129, 131, 132
porosity 17
potter's plaster 19

potter's slab 15,16, 18, 23
potter's wheel 12, 13, 16, 22, 23, 24, 25,
    26, 27, 32, 60, 128
pouring lips 76, 83
pouring spout 93, 94, 95, 96, 97
primary clay 10
profile cutter 75

raku 110, 129, 132, 133, 134
rotation 31, 32, 39

salt glaze 129, 137, 138, 139
scale 99, 100, 101, 103, 108, 109, 121, 127
secondary clay 10, 11, 13
sedimentary clay 11
Shand, Brian 26
shape 100, 103, 105, 106, 107, 108, 115,
    126, 131
shaping rib 44, 45, 51, 55, 56, 65, 67, 69,
    70, 94, 119
sieve 13, 14
slop 20
Soldner, Paul 24
spherical form 54, 55, 57, 60, 61,
    112–114, 117, 118, 120
sponge 44, 52
spout 93, 94, 95, 96, 97, 99
stamp 80
Stewart, Fergus 129, 137, 138, 139
stick sponge 44, 56
stoneware 129, 132, 140, 141, 142
surform 64

teapot 75, 92, 93, 94, 95, 96, 97, 98, 132
texture 100, 101, 102, 103, 107, 125
throwing 28, 39, 123, 142
throwing rings 54
throwing off the hump 84, 93 100, 101,
    103, 106, 107
tools 44
transitional point 53
trimming needle 44, 68, 94
turning or trimming 47, 71, 72, 75, 84,
    86, 89, 92, 95, 98, 124, 125

visual language 56, 111, 112, 128, 131
vitreous 17

wedging 20, 21, 22, 23
wheel head 24, 27, 31, 32, 34, 40, 46, 62,
    64, 66
wire 45, 95, 96